"Make It Home Before Dark"

"Make It Home Before Dark"

GOD'S CALL TO HOLINESS IN OUR WALK WITH HIM

CRAWFORD W. LORITTS, JR.

MOODY PRESS

CHICAGO

ISBN: 0-8024-5437-2

1 3 5 7 9 10 8 6 4 2

Printed in the United States of America

To Our Children:
Bryan, Korie, Heather, Bryndan, and Holly,
who are God's loving reminders that I am
responsible and accountable to them and their generation
to make it home before dark.

Contents

Acknowledgments

When I was a kid growing up in Newark, New Jersey, I never dreamed that I would one day be the author of anything, let alone several books. And imagine—people have actually read them! So, since you are holding this book in your hands, I want to thank you for even considering taking a look at these pages and the message God has placed on my heart to share with you.

This book is not just the product of a burden I have and a need I perceive, but it is also, in a very real sense, a team effort. First, I want to thank my friend and mentor Robertson McQuilkin whose life and godly leadership exemplify so much of what I have tried to say in this book. In fact, God used a prayer that he has written to lead me to more deeply ponder the issues related to repentance, and this book is part of my thinking and pilgrimage.

Karen and our children hold me accountable. The thought of betraying them and their trust in me constantly keeps me coming to the Cross for grace and strength to "stay the course" and pursue godliness and holiness. Their prayers, love, and encouragement have modeled grace to me and teach me that repentance is a wonderful provision and gift of God's amazing grace.

The people who have heard me preach and teach at churches and conferences over the past few years have taught me so much about the power of God to cleanse, transform, and give new beginnings to broken, repentant pilgrims. On more than a few occasions the tears have rolled down my cheeks as people have told me their stories of God's love, forgiveness, and mercy in their lives. They, too, have driven me to write this book.

The partnership and relationship that I enjoy with the Moody team is beyond wonderful. Jim Bell, Cheryl Dunlop, and Linda Haskins have made what God has placed on my heart a reality. I want to thank them for coming alongside me and helping me to identify my burdens. They have given me the platform and the wherewithal to say it.

And Steve Wamberg . . . he is the man! His ability to help me frame what I have to say and then put it in a clear, readable "package" has made all of the difference in the world. He is one of the most creative people I know.

I want to thank my Executive Assistant, Leonard ("Scottie") Scott. Scottie "directs the traffic" in my life and helps me to sort out the blizzard of activities, appointments, and requests. His servant spirit coupled with an eye for detail has helped me to stay on target. He has been invaluable in the process of pulling this book together.

Foreword

C rawford Loritts's call to repentance is not what you might expect. This is no evangelistic appeal to the sinner, but a wake-up call to the saint. It's a powerful call to adopt repentance as a way of life. This slim volume is strong medicine but . . .

- desperately needed

- winsomely offered

- powerfully illustrated

- biblically grounded

- verdict demanding

Although commonly held false ideas about the subject of repentance are clearly exposed, the thrust of this little volume is not primarily to correct our thinking. It's aimed rather at introducing us to the kind of abundant life every true believer longs for. And I can certify that our guide in that exciting quest is reliable. Crawford Loritts not only writes with passion; I've known him personally for many years and can testify that he lives what he preaches.

As a bonus, what makes this an exciting read is that the author is a twenty-first century communicator. "The most valued workers in the new century will be storytellers. Any professional—advertiser, teacher, politician, entrepreneur, athlete, or minister—will be valued for the ability to come up with stories that captivate an audience."[1]

That one young man could personally encounter so many horrific examples of Christian failure and magnificent examples of Christian success may surprise you, but the end result is there's no place to hide! So don't try, because if we'll only come out of hiding and follow Crawford Loritts's lead, we can experience the life of biblical promise. In fact, we'll surely get home before dark!

—Robertson McQuilkin
Columbia, S.C.
April 2000

NOTE

1. *The Futurist,* June 1996, 9.

Introduction

I have a great burden that I want to discuss in these pages. That burden is reflected in the following nine reasons for writing this book. In the words of my dear friend Bobb Biehl, these indeed are "the things that make me pound the table and weep" with regard to the whole issue of repentance.

First, *what is often passed off as repentance has nothing to do with what the Scriptures say repentance is.* This book is by no means a complete scholarly treatise on the nature of biblical repentance. But it is my prayer that as you read through these pages, God will speak to your heart and make clear the nature of repentance from a balanced biblical perspective.

Second, *we need authenticity in our walk and relationship with God.* We need to work on erasing the line between what we say and who we really are. We must return to authenticity. We must walk in reality. I believe that repentance is the key to opening and unlocking this reality. I believe genuine repentance will lead to the authenticity where Christ can be demonstrated in all of His beauty and all of His power. I believe that power is found through a humble, genuine, honest, transparent walk in relationship with Him.

Third, *I want to offer hope to discouraged, defeated pilgrims.* In my travels, I meet so many Christians who have been beaten down by sin and rejection in their lives. They scream out as the apostle Paul did in Romans 7:24, "Wretched man that I am! Who will set me free from the body of this death?" Through the pages of this book, as you read, I want to offer biblical hope to anyone who is struggling with life-controlling sin. I am here to remind you that whatever the issues are that bring discouragement and defeat to your life, there is hope.

Fourth, *I am writing this book to underscore the wonderful, positive nature of repentance.* We tend to view repentance as something dark, gloomy, and extremely painful. To be honest, the process of repentance can be very painful. It hurts to have to deal face-to-face with sin and disgrace. But it's also beautiful. Repentance opens the door to great joy, to great release. Burdens are lifted when there's true repentance.

Fifth, I want to underscore throughout this book that *repentance is the primary vehicle to both personal and corporate revival.* There can be no revival without the repentance of sin. No program or process in the Christian life can produce revival and renewal, no matter how good the Bible study program is, no matter how wonderful the outreach strategy may be, no matter how great the seminar or workshop that you attended may be. The key to all renewal, the key to all wholeness, the key to all awakening in the Christian life has to do with dealing directly and biblically with sin.

Sixth, *I want to speak to the destructive, false repentance of legalism.* Legalism is an extreme that keeps people in bondage. It's a tool of the Enemy that is prevalent throughout the body of Christ. Legalism is the archenemy of grace.

It fuels false guilt. It is rooted in rules and regulations and standards that cannot be supported by the Scriptures.

Seventh, *I want to identify and dispel some of the common barriers to true repentance.* In the pages that follow, we'll take a more detailed look at barriers to biblical repentance. We'll talk about what they are, how we need to deal with them, and how to get rid of them. In that way, we can get onto the path to wholeness and renewal.

Eighth, *I want to underscore the awesome majesty and holiness of our great God.* Truly, this is the ultimate reason to repent. In our popular approach to Christianity in our culture, God has been trivialized into a "bosom buddy" and a "lifelong pal." We have made God sort of a folk hero, and we have allowed the culture to relegate Him into that role. Therefore, we shouldn't be surprised that our "needs" now demand our first attention, nor that we have lost the awe and the respect and the reverence we once held for the God of the universe.

Finally, *I want to point toward the indescribable mercy and grace of God that is released and experienced through repentance.* Freedom is a great by-product of forgiveness. God wants His children to be full, free, and forgiven.

When I left the house as a teenager, my father always said, "Son, you make it home before dark." Sometimes that seemed like a restriction. But it also gave me great freedom to do the right thing. Because Dad made it eminently clear that I was accountable to him, his statement allowed me to avoid much that might have tempted me after the light was gone from the day.

In this book, I pray you'll begin to understand that repentance isn't a restriction, but the pathway to wholeness.

As God's children, let's all make it home before dark. Robertson McQuilkin wrote a prayer that I think can speak for all of us. I've quoted it here with his permission.

"LET ME GET HOME BEFORE DARK"

It's sundown, Lord. The shadows of my life stretch back into the dimness of the years long spent. I fear not death, for that grim foe betrays himself at last, thrusting me forever into life: life with You, unsoiled and free. But I do fear. I fear the dark specter may come too soon—or do I mean too late? I fear that before I finish I might stain Your honor, shame Your name, grieve Your loving heart. Few, they tell me, finish well. Lord, let me get home before dark.

Will my life show the darkness of a spirit grown mean and small, fruit shriveled on the vine, bitter to the taste of my companions, a burden to be borne by those brave few who love me still? No. Lord, let the fruit grow lush and sweet, a joy to all who taste, a spirit-sign of God at work, stronger, fuller. Brighter at the end. Lord, let me get home before dark.

Will it be the darkness of tattered gifts, rust-locked, half-spent, or ill-spent, a life that once was used of God now set aside? Grief for glories gone or fretting for a task God never gave? Mourning in the hollow chambers of memory, gazing on the faded banners of victories long gone? Cannot I run well until the end? Lord, let me get home before dark.

The outer me decays—I do not fret or ask reprieve. The ebbing strength but weans me from mother earth and grows me up for heaven. I do not cling to shadows cast by mortality. I do not patch the scaffold lent to build the real, eternal me. I do not clutch about me my cocoon, vainly struggling to hold hostage a free spirit pressing to be born.

But will I reach the gate in lingering pain—body distorted, grotesque? Or will it be a mind wandering untethered among light phantasies or grim terrors? Of Your grace, Father, I humbly ask . . . let me get home before dark.

CHAPTER ONE

Wholeness Versus Compartmentalization

A TALE OF TWO CHRISTIANS

Henry Jordan grew up in a Christian home. At an early age he made a decision to commit his life to Christ.

Henry and his family attended a wonderful church. It was full of great Christian activity and solid biblical teaching and was host to an exciting youth group. Henry took full advantage of that group as he grew up. He did "the whole thing": planned activities, missions trips, and summer camps alike.

After his graduation from high school, Henry attended a well-known Christian college where he majored in business administration and marketing. He excelled in college. In fact, he was considered a leader on the campus. Henry served as president of both his junior and senior classes, and was a member of several prestigious academic fraternities.

Henry entered the real estate business after college. Before long, he was a successful real estate developer. Within a relatively short period of time, Henry became a very

wealthy man. He became a community leader. He was involved in evangelistic outreaches. His company funded
various Christian initiatives, missionaries, and organizations. Henry was also an elder in his local church. He had
made major contributions to the church through years of
leadership and his generosity with his personal fortune.

Then tragedy caught up with Henry's personal life. The
community was shocked when they heard that Henry had
been caught with a high-priced call girl. The local newspa-
pers, radio, and TV covered the story.

The shame and embarrassment were almost too much
for Henry to handle.

When he was confronted by the leaders of the church,
Henry admitted that what he had done was wrong. Still, he
quickly began to make excuses for his sin. He even blamed
his wife for her "lack of warmth."

You see, Henry had lived with this problem for years—
and that was the problem. He had developed a private addiction to pornography, and he had never forsaken it. Rather,
Henry just "managed" it. Whenever he indulged in this
sinful activity, the shame hit him. Henry's response was to
privately "claim a verse," but he never seriously sought
help.

Pride stood in Henry's way. Oddly enough, as he "managed" the sin, it became increasingly unmanageable. His
appetite for sexual activity—and his desire to live out the
fantasies he read about—began to grow. Henry kept all of
this a big secret, of course. He acted out these fantasies
mostly when he was on out-of-town business trips. Away
from home, he indulged his sexual appetite with prosti-
tutes.

Henry was a bright man. So, through the years, he had
become adroit at manipulation. Not even his wife knew
this dark, private side of Henry. He felt trapped. He was
driven to keep his big secret because of his visibility and
his reputation as a Christian leader in the community.

Compartmentalized Christianity

After Henry was discovered and the news was out, some of his Christian friends had a "hindsight insight." They remembered that, despite his outgoing nature, Henry was evasive (sometimes even strangely silent) when the issues of accountability were raised. You see, Henry knew how to hide his sin. He could "keep it in the back," compartmentalize it, and still look like and act as if he was a wonderful, effective Christian.

Let's contrast Henry's story with that of Judy Hallsey. Judy is a thirty-four-year-old single parent with two children. Judy has been a Christian for just over six years. Prior to coming to Christ, she experienced a broken marriage to her high school sweetheart, Kevin.

The Hallseys' marriage started out as if it would last forever. Judy and Kevin were the ideal couple. They were both popular in high school, but shortly after the wedding things began to fall apart. Kevin wanted to spend more time with "the guys" than he did with Judy. It seemed as if he was running from something. Predictably, a noticeable distance developed between the two of them.

Kevin wasn't the only one at fault, however. Judy contributed to the breakup of the relationship too. Since childhood, Judy had engaged in a pattern of lying and dishonesty. For as long as she could remember—and for a variety of reasons—Judy had lied about almost everything. Judy's dishonesty as an adult drove a wedge in her relationship with Kevin. It fed Kevin's desire to spend more time with his friends than with his wife. Judy didn't tell the truth about where she was, what she did, or even what happened with their money. She constantly lied in an attempt to impress other people. Kevin sought refuge with his friends, never really knowing whether he got a straight story from Judy. Finally the distance between them overwhelmed their marriage, and they divorced.

The divorce left Judy an emotionally broken person. She carried an enormous amount of guilt because of her dishonesty. Although she tried to comfort herself by focusing on Kevin's neglect (and an assortment of his other faults and shortcomings), she still could not rid herself of the guilt and shame associated with the lies she had so often told.

Before long, Judy's sense of guilt and shame became almost unbearable. At times she felt totally hopeless and in the pit of despair. Then one day she ran into Beverly Hawkins, an old friend from high school, at her youngest son's baseball game. During the game they renewed their acquaintance and caught up on old times.

Judy was delighted to see Beverly once again. It had been quite a while. Over the next two weeks, they talked as they waited for their sons' practice to end. They talked throughout their sons' games. As the baseball season ended two weeks later, they made an appointment to meet again.

Beverly met Judy for coffee the following Saturday morning. In tears, Judy told of the pain that she was going through. Judy had not talked to anyone about the anguish that was in her heart since her marriage with Kevin had ended. Judy was somewhat embarrassed. Yet as she spoke, she also felt a great sense of relief and release. She poured her heart out to a dear friend. Beverly sat, listening to every word, empathizing with Judy.

Judy felt so much at ease. She felt as if she was drawn to Beverly's heart. In fact, she said to Beverly, "You know, I've been watching you these past few weeks ever since we reconnected at the ball game and, I have to say, I notice a difference in your life. You seem to be so much at peace. You're at ease with your life. The issues surrounding your life don't seem to upset you, either. I'd love to have what you have."

Beverly humbly thanked her. Then she confessed to Judy that she had not always had the peace that Judy wanted.

Beverly related to Judy how her older sister had explained the Gospel to her a few years after high school, and about her personal decision to receive Christ as her Savior and Lord. Beverly candidly recounted the changes, too, that Christ brought to her life.

You can guess what came next. Beverly went on to explain to Judy how she could establish that same relationship with Christ. Right there in the restaurant, Judy bowed her head and repeated a prayer after Beverly, expressing her faith in Christ.

Conversion, Confession, and Congruency

Too often, we evangelicals would let the story end there. But this point of decision is actually the beginning of the issues we're about to cover. Why? Because our decisions at conversion are rarely the end of our life experience. Our prayers to receive Christ don't always affect our behavior down the road, as we saw with Henry—and are about to see with Judy.

Judy left that coffee shop with a new sense of hope and direction. She felt a strange sense of cleanness about her life. Over the days and weeks ahead, Judy also developed a hunger and appetite for the Scriptures, and she began to grow in her newfound faith as a Christian. But she still struggled with lying. Each time she lied, she experienced guilt and conviction.

Judy mustered the courage to tell this embarrassing, sinful secret to Beverly. She wanted help, and so she asked for it, even though she wasn't sure how Beverly would react to her confession.

Beverly responded graciously when Judy told her of her ongoing struggle. But she didn't soft-pedal the severity of Judy's situation, either. Beverly invited Judy to become a part of an accountability group, a small group of women that met once a week. It sounds weird, but Judy's sensitivity to the Lord caused her to be honest to the three other women in the group about her lying. She learned not to hide her sin and sinfulness. In so doing, she has embraced repentance.

Judy's conversion led her to a new pattern of honest confession. That confession helped her life to hang together and make sense in ways it never had before. Her faith and her actions became more congruent. Now, the love and security she is experiencing in her relationship with the Savior and with the women in her accountability group are helping her overcome the sinful habit of lying. Judy still slips occasionally, but she makes it right. As a result, her lies are fewer and farther apart. She has learned that *darkness breeds destruction and light leads to life.*

Judy is now living at the crossroads of overcomers, where honesty before God and transparency with oneself and others intersect.

Our friend Henry played the tragic game of compartmentalizing his life. His pride would not allow him to own up to the truth of his struggle with sin. Quietly, in hiding, he eventually destroyed himself. In contrast, Judy allowed brokenness to drive her to a place of confession, repentance, and eventual wholeness.

"COMPARTMENTALIZING" DEFINED

Webster's Third International Dictionary defines *compartmentalize* as "to separate into compartments or categorize in a manner tending to preclude interrelationships." So when we compartmentalize, we put sin in an area of our lives that is hidden, so we think, from others. To compartmentalize sin simply means to hide it.

Our desire for this kind of "sin management" is often driven by self-deception. The sin is never dealt with. It is just quietly managed in such a way that it's kept out of obvious view. We think that "out of sight, out of mind" will apply to others' perception of our sin. Eventually, we ourselves are deceived into thinking that if our sin can be hidden, it must not be so big. We can even delude ourselves into thinking we're so good at "sin management" that God Himself can't see our trespasses.

When we compartmentalize, we push aside our sin into an area that we think is not related to other areas of our lives. We compartmentalize sermons too, in not allowing what we hear to interact with our weekday lives, and by forgetting what we have heard as soon as we walk outside the church doors. But as we'll see throughout the course of this book, our lives cannot be divided up into unrelated segments. Sin that is not repented of will always be exposed. It's a principle of the universe: *One way or the other, we'll have to deal with our sin.*

Henry lived to compartmentalize. Judy pursued wholeness. The difference in their two stories are not unlike the contrast between David and Saul in the Scriptures.

HOW DO KINGS DEAL WITH FAILURE?

David and Saul had some amazing similarities. They both were from small towns. They both had leadership thrust upon them when they were not looking for it. They both experienced great deliverance by the hand of God in battle. They both sinned and failed terribly.

Still, a major difference remained between them. David was known as "a man after [God's] own heart" (1 Samuel 13:14). Saul, however, was rejected as king for his repeated acts of disobedience and cowardice. David stayed on in the office even after he had committed adultery with Bathsheba and orchestrated a vicious deceitful plan to murder her husband Uriah and cover his tracks. (You can check into the full story in 2 Samuel 11 and 12.)

So what's the difference between Saul and David? The only explanation is that through all of David's failures, *he continued to fall at God's feet in brokenness, seeking cleansing and forgiveness.* He was sincere in his pursuit of righteousness. His walk with God was not a public relations game or a means to secure power and favor in the eyes of people. In a word, David was a *repenter.* David's words in Psalm 51 ring through the history of God's people—because we've all "been there" with him:

> Be gracious to me, O God, according to Your
>   lovingkindness;
> According to the greatness of Your compassion blot out
>   my transgressions. . . .
> Behold, You desire truth in the innermost being,
> And in the hidden part You will make me know
>   wisdom. . . .
> The sacrifices of God are a broken spirit;
> A broken and a contrite heart, O God,
> You will not despise. *(Psalm 51:1, 6, 17)*

As David repented, he recognized that God's plan for him was a restoration to wholeness, beginning with the truth about himself. He recognized that brokenness and repentance were the keys that opened the possibility of restoration—and that a forthright acknowledgment of his sin was the beginning of the entire process.

Not so with Saul. He was the master manipulator. His legendary ability to twist the facts finally was his undoing. He would not sincerely repent of his sin. He seemed to be constantly looking for ways to justify or hide his disobedience. The account of Saul's disobedience regarding the destruction of the Amalekites in 1 Samuel 15 offers a prime example of Saul's ability to compartmentalize. Saul was commanded to destroy the Amalekites and all their holdings. Instead, Saul spared their king and those things that he thought had some worth. When the prophet Samuel confronted Saul regarding his blatant disobedience, Saul twisted the facts about his motives. He said that the intent in sparing some of "the spoil" was to save it for a sacrifice to God.

At this point, can't you hear something in Saul's head saying, "Yeah, that's the ticket! We wanted to sacrifice them all along! What's the problem here?"

Samuel responded to Saul's "near-obedience" with these words:

> Has the Lord as much delight in burnt offerings and sacrifices as in obeying the voice of the Lord? Behold, to obey is better than sacrifice, and to heed than the fat of rams. For rebellion is as the sin of divination, and insubordination is as iniquity and idolatry. Because you have rejected the word of the Lord, He has also rejected you from being king. *(1 Samuel 15:22–23)*

Saul's stature as the king of Israel stood in the way of an honest, transparent walk with God. Much like Henry Jordan, he was more concerned about the favor and opinions of man than he was about the approval of God. Because he would not genuinely repent, he never experienced the forgiveness of God.

Saul's response to sin was to hide it. He had a complete program of private sin management, in fact, and compartmentalizing was the key to his program.

THE PURSUIT OF WHOLENESS

In contrast to compartmentalization, wholeness drives us to pursue honesty and integrity. "Wholeness" is not perfection; it does not mean that we have arrived. But true repentance brings an openness to all of our hearts and lives that marks the journey to wholeness.

Webster's Third International Dictionary defines *wholeness* as "the quality or state of being whole; an unreduced or unbroken completeness or totality; a hale vigor or soundness: integrity." *And that's what we need to pursue.*

I want to make clear that a Christian's journey to wholeness takes a lifetime to complete. Having said that, we must also take the steps we can each day. We dare not take the time God gives us for granted. For many of us, only the finest of lines separates our working hard at our profession from becoming a full-blown workaholic. The hours we spend to provide for our families can too often extend into hours we rob from them. Our spouses are sometimes uncomfortable bringing the issue to our attention. Our children usually aren't.

That's exactly the situation that faced Jeff, an up-and-coming young executive in a Fortune 500 company. Jeff had been a Christian since his high school years, when he invited Christ to be his Savior and Lord at a Fellowship of Christian Athletes camp. Jeff had met his college sweetheart, Kelley, at a campus fellowship group at the state university they both attended. Jeff and Kelley set some goals before they were married: how much family income they wanted to gross annually, in which neighborhood they wanted to buy their first house, which stocks they would buy to build their retirement portfolio, even the country club they wanted to join in Atlanta. Strangely, their spiritual goals were left unstated at the time.

Jeff was a climber in the company. He had a promising future by everyone's reckoning. Kelley was the ever-faithful wife. She taught as a substitute for "pin money" until she gave birth to their first son, Derek, almost five years to the day after they were married.

Once Jeff began climbing that corporate ladder, he became protective of his position and his goals. That meant more hours at the office, more hours working at home, and less time watching Derek grow.

Another five years, and Derek was ready for kindergarten. Jeff was about to be named a senior vice-president—the youngest one in his company's history. He had a lock on their future, even though it would mean the same kind of dedication and hours it had taken to bring him to this point in his career. Jeff and Kelley had achieved their goals: the dream house, the right neighborhood, the growth stocks, the country club. They'd even become part of a church some of the other senior executives attended.

Jeff was making his typical dash out the door as Derek ate breakfast one day—the first day Derek would attend school. Derek turned to him and asked, "Daddy, will you take me to school today?"

Jeff wished he could have. If he'd only thought about it, he could have postponed his 8:30 meeting until 10:00. He smiled sadly as he ruffled his son's hair. "Sorry, buddy. I know it's a huge day for you, but I have a meeting even before you have to be at school."

Derek didn't give up. "Daddy, will you pick me up when it's time to come home?"

Now guilt was entering into Jeff's gut, and he wasn't sure he liked it. "Aw, Son, I wish I could." There was that 3:00 he could have shifted to 2:00 if he'd only known it would matter so much to Derek.

"Daddy, now that I'll be in school all day, will I be so busy that I'll never see you again?"

"Of course not. We'll see each other."

"But when? If you can never get away from work to see me, and they won't let me leave school, and you have to work even when you're here at home, *when?*"

Jeff looked at Derek, whose eyes were filling up. He glanced across the kitchen at Kelley, who seemed dumbstruck at Derek's question. Jeff made an on-the-spot decision.

"Son, I'll be there to pick you up after school. I'll have to change one appointment to do that, but I'll make it happen."

And he did. Just as important, Jeff kept making the adjustments that let his family know that they held priority over his career. Derek saw more of Jeff during that kindergarten year than he had in his first five years of life combined. Jeff had repented of putting his job before his family. He was still successful, but he quit climbing and started living. It didn't take long for Kelley to appreciate the wisdom of that change, either.

Derek entered his teenage years with the foundation only an involved father can bring to a child. Jeff and Kelley didn't have as much in their portfolio as they might have had with Jeff on the fast track at the office, but the investment they'd made in Derek was priceless.

Remember, then, that it's true that you probably have a lifetime to work through the complete process of repentance and change. Still, those you love most will benefit from the steps of repentance and change you can make *today*.

We need to pursue wholeness. How we live must tell the truth about who we are. Again, repentance brings about a certain openness, an appropriate vulnerability that is the arena for God's activity in and through our personal lives. Remember when you were new to the faith? You were willing to let God work in you in ways you may not be comfortable thinking about today.

There's a reason for that: *We have created an environment in Christian circles that makes it difficult for people to be real and genuine.* Because we have to look like winners, we're afraid to acknowledge our sinfulness in areas in which we struggle. So we learn quickly how to play the game, and we withdraw to our corners.

Then we compartmentalize. We destroy ourselves, usually with each one quietly whimpering to ourselves about "what might have been," when God's desire for us from the moment of our redemption is to make us whole.

Jesse Bingham grew up in a wonderful, warm Christian home. His father was an outstanding pastor in the community where he lived. Therefore, Jesse was exposed to some of the finest Christian teaching in the country. He had been a part of the most wonderful Christian experiences imaginable.

Although he made a profession of faith as a young teenager, Jesse began to rebel as he grew older. He had always been strong willed. The time came when he was simply determined to do whatever he wanted to do. Through his teen years he experimented with drugs and alcohol. He wandered far from home. Many, many people prayed for Jesse as he experienced one setback after another.

The heartache and heartbreak that he brought to his parents were unimaginable. At times he would apologize, "confess his sin," and seek to get right. But it was clear there was a deep struggle in his soul.

One day, Jesse decided to carjack a student's car. The young fellow gave Jesse the keys to the car without a struggle. As the student was walking away from the car, Jesse shot him in the back and killed him.

Jesse was arrested, tried, and sentenced to spend the rest of his life in jail. I went by to visit him there not long ago. As I talked with Jesse, he said these words to me: "You know, I'm so terribly sorry for what I've done and the pain that I've caused. I know the disappointment I've been to my parents, and the pain that I caused this young man's family . . . and I'm so terribly sorry."

Tears filled Jesse's eyes as he continued. "Although I'm behind bars here, there's a freedom that I'm experiencing now that I've never known before. I'm sorry for what I've done, and I've asked God to forgive me. *I'm beginning to experience that forgiveness.*"

You see, that forgiveness was released when Jesse finally came to the end of himself and experienced the joy of repentance. It is my prayer, as you wander through the pages of this book, that you'll discover that that degree of joy and release can be yours. Until that happens, you're even more of a prisoner than Jesse.

Don't let your compartment for sin become your prison. Unlock it; confess it—and get on with your journey to integrity and wholeness.

CHAPTER TWO

Isolation Versus Community

One of the great joys and privileges of my ministry is to have the occasional opportunity of speaking to prisoners.

Those of you who have ever had that experience know exactly what I mean. In most prisons, there is a growing, dynamic Christian community that actively seeks to reach and disciple fellow inmates for Christ. That story is not often seen or told in the media. That's sad, because some of the most honest, transparent Christians I've ever met are inmates.

What produces this kind of character among prisoners who become Christians? I suppose their surroundings constantly remind them of their sin. Many of them are broken people. They've come to grips with what they have done wrong. After coming to faith in Christ—and receiving true forgiveness and cleansing—they display a remarkable degree of transparency. They have nothing left to lose by being honest before God and each other. So it is indeed a joy for me to minister to this community of responsive brothers and sisters in the body of Christ.

I must tell you that each time I minister at a prison, I

receive far more than I give. I am humbled and impressed by what God is doing among inmates across the country.

None of this denies the reality of penitentiary life. Obviously, not everybody who is behind bars is converted. The disruptions that take place in prisons have been well-chronicled. Rape, robbery, and violent assault alike are a part of the everyday picture in many prisons. And as the old saying goes, every inmate knows that in order to survive he has to "watch his back."

Some think that one of the most effective ways of dealing with inmates who are unruly is to place them in solitary confinement or isolation. In isolation there's virtually no contact with anyone. It is hoped that without human contact the inmate will deeply ponder his errant ways and emerge a better person. The thinking goes, "Now that this prisoner has had time alone to contemplate what he has done, he will have a sense of remorse and regret. He'll turn around. 'Solitary' will serve as a searing reminder that he mustn't ever again do what he did."

Too often, just the opposite happens. Separated from human contact, an inmate's mind can play tricks on him. Reality is distorted. A prisoner's ability to think rationally is greatly diminished. There's no one to "bounce things off." There's no one else to give him a context for thoughts, feelings, and actions.

As a result, some prisoners emerge from solitary confinement *permanently* isolated, both emotionally and mentally. Their distortions of reality become entrenched. They become hardened. They question the realities around them. They no longer fit in. They bear the marks of a back-fired time-out session.

CHOOSING ISOLATION: SELF-IMPOSED "SOLITARY"

Don't get me wrong. Isolation is not always a bad thing. Sometimes it's good to get alone and put things in perspective. Sometimes we must go off alone (with God, I hope) to think through issues, to push out the clutter that invades our minds and confuses our perspective. That kind of isolation has been a habit of mine for a number of years. About once a month, I take a complete day and go away to some quiet place. I take that time to be alone with God and weigh issues in my life, my ministry, and my family. I usually emerge from those times of isolation refreshed and ready to meet the challenges around me.

That's not the kind of isolation we're talking about in this chapter. Instead, we'll discuss the dangerous isolation that creeps into our souls when we refuse to deal with life issues and problems. This is a negative, destructive isolation. It is an unwholesome detachment from others. It's choosing to be alone because others remind a person of what he or she has failed to confront and deal with.

This is a self-imposed solitary confinement. It is a form of self-deception that says we would much rather "enjoy" the imprisonment of our sin than to live in open, honest community with others. Unless we break free through genuine repentance, we assign ourselves to this negative, permanent isolation. Its result is further self-deception, further distortion and rejection of truth, and a consequent case of "spiritual insanity."

We choose isolation because it minimizes the effects of others on us. We choose isolation because, then, we don 't have to confront the sin that has such a strong hold on us.

The Dangerous "Safety Zone"

When I speak of isolation I am not necessarily referring only to those people who totally withdraw from others. Quite the contrary, I've known of men and women who have been secretly engaged in all manner of sin who spend a lot of time around Christians. In fact, they go to Bible studies and fellowship groups regularly—yet they live in isolation. They have certain sides of their lives to which they let others get close. Even so, they protect themselves.

It's really a question of transparency and vulnerability. We can be around people, involved in their lives, and still live in emotional and spiritual isolation. How do we do that? *By guarding and protecting the areas in which we're most vulnerable.*

We shrink back from any meaningful interaction with regard to those areas of sin or weakness. That kind of interaction might be too close to home. It could even reveal us for what we are. So we selectively let people into the safe areas of our lives. We give the appearance of great openness and vulnerability, but in reality we're hiding the truth from them—and ultimately from ourselves.

Isolation, therefore, is not simply withdrawal from people. It is the more subtle effort to hide and deny the truth while playing our wonderfully deceptive "fellowship" games.

Neither is this call to transparency a suggestion that we inappropriately tell our sin and struggles to any and every Christian we happen to meet. We must use discretion in what we disclose, and to whom. Still, this is a call to open our hearts and our lives to those who are lovingly committed to us and who are willing to be honest with us in calling sin by its true name. We must put biblical honesty and integrity into action.

Into Hiding, Away from the Truth

I believe God is calling for all of us to tear down our hideouts and move into our primary places of residence in His community of believers. I also believe answering that call won't be easy. Our pattern of running and hiding is nothing new. It's a part of our spiritual DNA, in fact. Our insidious natural tendency is noted well in the old hymn "Come, Thou Fount of Every Blessing":

Prone to wander, Lord, I feel it,

Prone to leave the God I love.

Our grandparents Adam and Eve magnificently demonstrated this tendency right after they both had sinned by disobeying God:

They heard the sound of the Lord God walking in the garden in the cool of the day, and the man and his wife hid themselves from the presence of the Lord God among the trees of the garden. Then the Lord God called to the man, and said to him, "Where are you?" He said, "I heard the sound of You in the garden, and I was afraid because I was naked; so I hid myself." And He said, "Who told you that you were naked? Have you eaten from the tree of which I commanded you not to eat?" The man said, "The woman whom You gave to be with me, she gave me from the tree, and I ate." Then the Lord God said to the woman, "What is this you have done?" And the woman said, "The serpent deceived me, and I ate." *(Genesis 3:8–13)*

My dear friend Joseph Garlington, pastor of Covenant Church of Pittsburgh, Pennsylvania, makes the observation that when God asks a question, He's not looking for information. More often than not, He wants us to face the truth about ourselves. When God said to Adam and Eve, "Where are you?" He was holding up a mirror to them and saying, "Look at yourselves. I've come out here to meet with you, and you have run from Me. You're hiding from Me."

Isolation was the very first response to God when Adam and Eve sinned. Their shame caused them to run from God. Perhaps in some perverse way, they thought that they could keep their disobedience to themselves. They chose isolation over repentant communion with God.

Regrettably, through the ages, this has been the typical response of mankind. We shut down and retreat into ourselves rather than embrace our failure and go to the source of cleansing, forgiveness, and help. Our shame ought to drive us to cry out for mercy and grace. So often, however, it pushes us toward the warped and pathetic self-preservation that is marked by isolation. This kind of response is a painfully accurate portrait of pride.

OUT OF THE TOY CHEST:
FIVE CHOICES TO FACE THE TRUTH

When our oldest daughter Heather was two years old, she committed some act that required Karen, my wife, to discipline her. Rather than facing up to the consequences of her action, Heather decided to run down to the family room, away from her mother. There, she hid in the toy chest.

Karen had to respond as a parent should. Even at that moment, though, it was a hilarious situation. Karen knew exactly where Heather was. She quietly followed Heather into the family room and waited. Our family toy chest is not opaque. You can see right through it. So Karen stood watching Heather through the toy chest. Heather didn't realize that her mother was in the room with her. For a few moments, Karen struggled to hide her laughter. Then she finally said to Heather, "Heather, what are you doing in that toy chest?"

Karen knew the answer. It was obvious what Heather was doing in the toy chest. Still, Karen wanted Heather to own up to what she had done and to embrace the reality of the fact that she was running away from the inevitable.

There have been times in my life when I have chosen to run to the toy chest rather than embrace the reality of what I've done. In those times, my heavenly Father has lovingly and patiently stood there and asked me, "Crawford, where are you?"

I believe that other contributing factors drive us to

choose isolation over community. I want to take a look at five of these reasons.

Avoiding Transparency

First, *some of us are by nature private people.* We are not naturally drawn to relationships. Some of us must work very hard to include others in our lives. Opening our hearts to others doesn't come easily. We have to intentionally work on transparency. We may understand that God never intended for us to live alone, but the private nature of our personalities makes it difficult to open up.

I say "we" and "our" advisedly. I tend to fall into this category. Despite the fact that I speak a great deal, have a public ministry, and am always around people, I cherish times to be alone. Often the way that I deal with issues and problems is to shrink back a little bit and try to think things through.

Though I'm no recluse, solitude has become a good friend of mine. But I have learned through the years that there are times in which solitude is my biggest enemy. If I let my desire to isolate myself control every response, it could hurt me in the long run. I had to learn, and continue to learn, how to open up my heart and my life to others. I believe that I am a better person, and, most importantly, a better Christian, because of learning to do what I naturally would shrink back from doing.

I want to encourage you—especially if you're a "soul mate" of mine in terms of a preference for privacy—to ask God to give you the courage and the strength to seek others out and to include them in your life. As we'll see later, God never intended for any of us to live solely unto ourselves, listening only to our own advice.

Avoiding Hurt

Second, *some of us choose isolation because we have been hurt or betrayed.* We have trusted our hearts and our confidences with someone, only to discover later that what we told was either used against us or inappropriately passed on to others. So we react and withdraw to isolation. We say to ourselves, "I've been burned, *and it will never happen again.*"

I can't tell you the number of people—those I know and who are close to me—who have been down this road. Unfortunately, I have been "up close and personal" with this kind of betrayal and hurt too.

Here is an issue of delicate balance: *We need to be open, but we also need to be wise.* We need to be extremely careful about the people to whom we allow close access to our hearts. We must choose wisely and pray about the people with whom we confide our struggles.

Just because a person is in a position of spiritual authority, say a pastor or another Christian leader, does not necessarily mean that that person deserves the disclosure of your heart either. A good friend of mine is a member of a prominent church. The pastor is well known, but he is enormously insecure and, quite frankly, full of himself. He does not know the difference between appropriate biblical authority and controlled manipulation of people. The lethal combination of insecurity and arrogance has driven this man to demand that those that are around him tell him their innermost struggles and areas of sin and temptation. Then he uses this information to keep them in line. That is, they must agree with and endorse whatever he chooses to do, without any question, or be subject to a form of blackmail through public embarrassment. This pastor has very subtle ways of reminding people of what he knows about them.

No question about it: This is one sick situation. Sadly, too, this is more common than we'd like to admit. The ranks of the ministry and Christian "leadership" has more than its share of manipulative egomaniacs who are self-deceived. These people of position are, at best, confused about the nature of true biblical leadership.

Avoiding Rejection

Third, *we choose isolation because we have experienced rejection.* Some of us have confessed our sin and failure to those close to us only to find that they cannot handle it. We become such a source of embarrassment and disappointment to them that they emotionally push us away. They avoid us because, in their minds, not only have we failed, but also we are failures. We are relational lepers. We make them look bad.

So many of us Bible-believing Christians are guilty of distancing ourselves from those who have confessed a moral failure. We take verses and passages out of context and use them as a means to camouflage our real hidden motives. We say things like, "God can never use that person again. Do you see how they messed up? They've really dragged the name of Christ through the mud. They've really hurt the cause of the kingdom!"

To be sure, all sin is hideous and terrible. (In a later chapter I will address this issue more fully.) However, we must be careful that we do not pervert the Scriptures to cover over our real motivation for distancing ourselves from those who confess moral failure or sin: our own personal sense of embarrassment.

Time and again, people have said to me in private that they would be afraid to go public with sin that they have committed. They fully understood their need to come clean through public confession. *But they were afraid of what Christians would do to them.* These "should-be confessees" anticipated that the Christians they knew would walk away and reject them.

This is a point of interest to me. As I've studied the Scriptures, God rushes toward us when we mess up and own up to it. But as I've studied the church, Christians often run away from repentant sinners.

Our desire to run from embarrassment can strike

painfully close to home. I know of one Christian leader whose daughter became pregnant out of wedlock. The young lady experienced genuine repentance and brokenness. She came before the church to ask for forgiveness. She owned up completely to the sin that she had committed. Still, her father wanted her out of his sight. He warned his daughter not to spend time with any of his friends—or anyone else who knew that she was his daughter.

Any father would feel wrenching pain, shame, and embarrassment in this situation. However, this man's response was ultimately devastating. The message that he sent to his family and friends is this: "Don't ever acknowledge doing anything that might make *me* look bad. Otherwise, I'll banish you too."

When we reject repentant, broken people, we assign them to isolation.

Avoiding Effort

Fourth, *sometimes we're drawn toward isolation simply by default.* We don't know what the Bible teaches about the relationship between individual sin and the joy of living in community with the rest of the body of Christ. In a very real sense, that's what this entire book is about.

Chuck Colson, chairman of Prison Fellowship and former White House counsel to President Nixon, has said that if you have God as your Father, then you must have the church as your mother. In other words, a commitment to Christ means that we have become a part of a new community called the body of Christ—the church. We are brothers and sisters. To a large degree, our sanctification depends upon our relationships with each other. We help each other, encourage each other, support each other; we rally around our wounded and nurture them back to health and wholeness. We are responsible for each other. When one hurts, we all hurt. When one falls, we are all sad. We are to rush to the repentant and love them back to full, complete restoration. When one of our members refuses to repent, we take no pleasure in that person's judgment and discipline.

We have all heard and perhaps even used the expression that "blood is thicker than water." The blood of Christ binds us together with ties that are eternal—yes, stronger even than some of our earthly family relationships. We are members of the same family. We want each family member to succeed, to "be all that we can be" in the Lord's army. Just as we invest time and energy into helping our family members develop into whole people, the body of Christ is designed to invest in helping each member fulfill his or her God-given potential.

My parents, who are now both with the Lord, ingrained in each of their children that home was more than just a house. Home is a community. Home is the last line of defense. Home is where people who live together and share together take care of each other.

Karen and I have four wonderful children. Through the years we have said repeatedly to them, "No matter what happens, we will always love you." That love is not some sentimental feeling. That love means that we are committed to their growth and development, including helping them to overcome and face their failures and sins. We stand with them to encourage them to be all that God wants them to be.

Is the family of God called to do any less? Of course not. The church is God's family and His community. "Community" means simply "where we live, and what we share in common." In fact, the word "common" is a root word for "community."

The church is God's community in this world. Among many other things, it is God's intention to demonstrate to a watching world what His character and nature are like through relationships between members of His community. The truth of the matter is, sometimes there's more community demonstrated in our civic clubs and the local bar than there is in our churches.

Look at these biblical snapshots as to how God's community should operate:

1 Thessalonians 5:14—We're to admonish, encourage, and help each other.

Jude 23—We should urgently snatch errant members "out of the fire."

James 5:16—We need to confess our faults and failures to one another and pray for each other.

Matthew 18:15—We're to go after those brothers and sisters who have wandered away from community and win them back.

1 Corinthians 12:26—As members of this community, this body, we identify with each other's sufferings and honors alike.

Ephesians 4:32—We must be kind, tenderhearted, and forgiving of one another.

You get the idea here. A premium is placed on preserving the unity and integrity of the community of God in our world.

One of the most powerful demonstrations of God's community in action that I witnessed was in 1995 at our Campus Crusade for Christ National Staff Conference. At Mobey Gymnasium at Colorado State University in Fort Collins, Colorado, more than four thousand Christian workers gathered for an address given by Nancy Leigh DeMoss of Life Action Ministry.

Nancy's message was powerful and riveting. However, something unusual happened when she came to a section of her message where she outlined the differences between "broken people" and "proud people." As she gave point-by-point contrasts, a holy hush fell over the entire audience. Quietly, but discernibly, people began to weep. Then outright sobbing broke out before Nancy could finish her message.

Spontaneously, for the next two days, people began to stream forward to confess their sin. After each confession, something totally unorchestrated happened. My life will never be the same having witnessed this incredible sight. Fellow staff members, as many as fifteen to twenty, would rush to the repentant sister or brother. They'd embrace that person and pray for him or her, loving the person to wholeness. They became a visible, tangible expression of our God's tremendous love and forgiveness.

That scene is forever burned into my heart and mind as a monumental demonstration of biblical community at work. Lives were changed and cleansed because God's body ran to—not from—the confessing members of His community.

Avoiding Honesty

There's a final reason that we choose isolation: Some of us are simply insincere. We don't want another change encounter with God. We have been living a lie for so long that we honestly do not know the truth from the lie. Sin has become deeply rooted and habitual. As we discussed in the first chapter, we have compartmentalized our sin. We have ignored the promptings of the Spirit of God and other warnings for so long that our hearts have grown cold, hard, and insensitive.

When we are in this condition, we seldom—if ever— experience the guilt associated with our sin and rebellion. In the words of the apostle Paul in 1 Timothy 4:2, our consciences have been "seared . . . as with a branding iron."

That's quite a picture. It's as though the nerve endings of our souls no longer sense the tender drawing of the Spirit of God. We no longer hear His call to repent. We have rationalized the behavior surrounding our sins so much and so often that we have not only deceived others, but we have deceived ourselves as well.

I know a man in ministry who has lied for many years about his ministry credentials. He has also been less than honest regarding the schools and degrees he lists on his résumé. He has fooled a lot of people. Yet he has been recognized as a national Christian leader, and held an unusual number of ministry positions in various churches and Christian organizations. It seems, though, that whenever friends and colleagues get close to him, he receives another "calling" and off he goes.

His flight away from one situation left him thinking everything was all right. Instead, he became further entrenched in his self-deception and even more isolated from genuine community. When the truth was revealed and he was confronted with his lies, he shrugged it off and treated the whole thing as if it were no big deal. His insincerity had unplugged his heart. To this very day, I don't know whether or not he has experienced genuine repentance.

Throughout this book I want to underscore this: *The way to maintain vital community and wholeness in our relationship with our Savior is to embrace repentance both as an identity and a lifestyle.*

At this point, then, let's identify our working definition of "repentance." Descriptively speaking, repentance is not simply sorrow concerning sin, although it does involve sorrow. Repentance is not repayment for sin, although we must seek to make things right and to make restitution whenever and wherever possible. Repentance is not reformation or "turning over a new leaf." It does not say, "I'll try to do better next time." No, repentance is described with the great New Testament Greek word *metanoia,* which literally means "a change of mind and attitude concerning our sin; a deliberate walking away from sin, once having seen its effects, toward the good."

Again, repentance is more than just how we think about sin or our attitude toward sin. It has to do with a new direction. I like what Richard Owen Roberts said in his book *Revival:*

> First and foremost, repentance is not a single thought or act. Repentance is not something once done and forever accomplished. Repentance is an ongoing process. One must be forever repentant. It is not enough to have once felt sorrow over sin. No single change of mind will suffice. No individual act of self-abasement will meet the biblical requirement. True repentance affects the whole person, alters the entire lifestyle and does not cease. True repentance is driven by an understanding of the nature and devastation of sin.

And that's what we want to take a look at in the next chapter.

CHAPTER THREE

Sin's Stain

A few years ago, my friend Dr. E. V. Hill invited me to preach at the church where he pastors, Mt. Zion Missionary Baptist Church in Los Angeles. Just before the evening service, I had a tremendous craving for some barbecue. We went to a barbecue restaurant not too far from Mt. Zion Missionary Baptist and had the most delicious barbecue I had ever tasted.

That meal was not without incident, however. I was wearing a very light-colored tie. The restaurant staff commented on that lovely light-colored tie, and they kindly offered their customary bibs to protect my clothing from potential barbecue-eating hazards. Clearly, they were experienced in this area.

Rather than accept any of the bibs they graciously offered, though, I thought to myself, *No, I won't make a mess.* With that thought, it was as though a magnetic force began drawing the barbecue sauce from my plate to that light-colored tie and the shirt upon which it rested. I spilled barbecue sauce all down the front of my tie and my shirt. It was one horrible, nasty mess. I tried everything to get the stain out. I put cold water on my tie and shirt, but the stain was stubborn and it wouldn't come out. I rubbed the ice cubes from my water glass on the stain. Nothing doing.

To add insult to injury, the stain was so high up on my tie that when I buttoned my suit jacket, it didn't hide anything. The stain was there for everybody to see. And because we were running a little late, I didn't have time to change my shirt or tie. We had to hustle back to the church.

I walked into the church and up onto the platform, stained tie and all. That evening as I stood before the congregation, I had to confess that my ruined tie was the product of a delicious barbecued meal. They had a great laugh with me, and I went ahead and preached that evening with my stains in full view.

THE PROBLEM: A FATAL STAIN

We are all marked with another stain that is no laughing matter. It's also a stain in full view: sin. It is in need of constant cleansing. That's why the promise of 1 John 1:7 is so crucial to each one of us: "But if we walk in the Light as He Himself is in the Light, we have fellowship with one another, and the blood of Jesus His Son cleanses us from all sin."

The reason we are in constant need of the cleansing power of the blood of Jesus is this: Sin's presence is never completely extricated from us as long as we're this side of heaven.

Our world is now familiar with the notoriously deadly disease called AIDS. There is no cure for this disease. It can be slowed, but the end result of AIDS is certain—death. The most conservative projections by the end of 1995 said there were more than 500,000 diagnosed cases of AIDS in the United States. Worldwide the count stood at over 1.3 million cases of AIDS. Yet another 20 million people worldwide are thought to be infected with HIV (human immunodeficiency virus), which leads to AIDS.

HIV infects and reproduces in the white blood cells of the human body. When body fluids—primarily blood and sexual fluids—that contain infected blood cells are introduced into otherwise healthy people, they can become infected with HIV too. After a few months, blood tests show them to be HIV-positive.

HIV gradually destroys the body's immune system as it commandeers white blood cells to reproduce itself. After it reproduces, it destroys the T-4 cells, releasing HIV particles to infect new cells and to repeat the cycle. This destruction occurs slowly. It can take more than a decade before the immune system is weak enough for the symptoms of illness to occur. When the first general symptoms appear, the infected person is said to be "HIV-positive symptomatic" (HIV-infected with the symptoms).

We dread AIDS, and rightly so. Yet we should dread the stain of sin even more. Sin affects the entire human race. Sin is even more deadly than AIDS, for it produces eternal damnation and separation. Unlike AIDS, there is a cure for sin. Yet the cure itself is deadly; God sent His Son once and for all to deal with the problem of sin and its effects. The writer of Hebrews said,

> But now once at the consummation of the ages, He has been manifested to put away sin by the sacrifice of Himself. And inasmuch it is appointed for men to die once and after this comes judgment, so Christ also, having been offered once to bear the sins of many, will appear a second time for salvation without reference to sin, to those who eagerly await Him. *(Hebrews 9:26–28)*

If we have trusted Christ as Savior and Lord, then this passage means that sin has been dealt with in our lives. In other words, we will never be separated eternally from the Lord Jesus. We'll be in God's presence when we pass from this life to the next. That's because when He died on that cross in our place and for our sin, Jesus Christ took care of the penalty of sin.

But sin can't be ignored in everyday life. Even for Christians, the presence of sin is very much with us. It lingers around us; it hovers over us; it trips us up. It can control us. Sin is a grand dilemma—and a deadly disease. That's why we need to understand the nature of sin and its stain. Biblical repentance, the means to "make it home before dark" and instead operate in the light of God, demands it.

What Is Sin Like?

Precisely what is sin? Let's keep it simple. In both the Old and New Testaments, "sin" implies moral deviation. Sometimes sin actually means *an act or deed that is contrary to God's ways.* It means we know what is right to do according to God's standards, and then we refuse to do it. Literal translations of both Old and New Testament words for sin read "missing the mark."

Sin can also mean *a power or principle that is contrary to God's will.* In this application, sin is not simply an act of the will, but a position of rebellion against God. As such, sin carries a power to influence not only the present decision to do wrong, but also the course of one's life to continue to do wrong.

Sin has an impact on our lives as Christians. It's ironic to me that although sin is at the root of the human predicament, we shun discussing it. It's not popular to talk about sin. It's uncomfortable to consider it. It doesn't win people to us. It's not a "message that sells." And yet, unless we wrestle with and honestly look at the horror of our devastating disease, we will not be able to effectively appropriate, much less apply, the cure.

Why Is Sin a Problem?

Let's start our "wrestling match" here: God is the Lawgiver. His righteous statutes and principles are the Law. Sin violates God's Law. In this area—think of it as the legal aspect of sin—sin is everything in the disposition, purpose, and conduct of man that is contrary to the express will (the Law) of God (the Lawgiver).

Take a hard look at that. Attitudes and actions, power and principle—sin covers all that ground. I'd like to discuss five things that combine to make sin a huge problem for each one of us.

God the Lawgiver has made clear the difference between right and wrong. If we're honest with ourselves, we'll recognize how familiar we are with the sad truth of James 4:17: "Therefore, to one who knows the right thing to do and does not do it, to him it is sin." Here's the bottom line, and our first big problem with sin: Our struggle with sin is rarely a struggle to figure out what is right. It's a struggle to do what we know is right in the first place, according to God's Law.

There's a second aspect to remember about sin. The "sinfulness of sin" lies in the fact that it is against God, even when the wrong we do is to others and ourselves. This is a very important observation. You see, God established the laws that govern life. I'm speaking specifically concerning God's revelation: The Word of God is not the product of other people; it's the product of God. So when I do something that damages someone else in violation of God's Word, it is not simply a wrong against that person. I have also violated God's law.

Third, sin is portrayed in the Bible as a real and active evil. Sin is not represented in the Bible as the absence of good, or as an illusion that stems from our human limitations. Sin is not just some nebulous weakness or human frailty. Sin is more than unwise, "it feels good so do it," out-of-control behavior that produces sorrow and distress. Sin is *active* rebellion against God's standard of righteousness.

That leads to a disturbing result, which is our fourth big problem with sin: Sin completely disrupts our relationship with God. Since God demands righteousness, sin is the faithless rebellion of the creature against the just authority of his Creator.

Our fifth big problem is that sin haunts us from the moment of our conception. Sin is a contradiction to the holiness of God, whose image we bear. As such, it brutally corrupts the nature we were created to have. The violation of God's law in our thoughts, words, and deeds shows the sinfulness in our hearts from childhood. This depraved condition is called "original sin" because it stems from Adam and Eve's first sin in the Garden of Eden.

We would be hopeless in any struggle against the big problem of sin had God not provided the ultimate solution.

Big Problem, Bigger Solution

Against this catastrophic backdrop of sin and its reality, the Gospel comes screaming as the good news of the deliverance that God has provided through His Son. Jesus bears the penalty of sin in place of His people: "For even the Son of Man did not come to be served, but to serve, and to give His life a ransom for many" (Mark 10:45).

You see, God's big solution for the big problem of sin was to buy mankind away from sin's power through the finished work of the cross of Jesus Christ.

Jesus also redeems us from lawlessness. He makes us long for good works and service to God and others. He offers a genuine solution to both the *actions* and *attitudes* of sin: "Who gave Himself for us to redeem us from every lawless deed, and to purify for Himself a people for His own possession, zealous for good deeds" (Titus 2:14).

Praise His holy name! But how do I apply all of this to my daily experience? How do I overcome the sin that I struggle with from day to day? How do I experience Christ's victory on a practical daily basis?

Glad you asked! The apostle Paul, I believe, answered

these questions in direct fashion. That's why we'll take a closer look at Romans chapters 6–8 in the pages that follow. A number of years ago when I began to understand and apply the truths found in these chapters of Scripture, my life changed dramatically. I began to understand that I did not have to live a defeated Christian life—a roller-coaster experience, if you will—in my walk and relationship with the Savior. I was liberated when this passage showed me that my position in Christ is not theoretical. It has powerful, practical implications that can help anyone to overcome sin this side of heaven.

You can know that same kind of victory too. Your first step is to accept the *proposition* Paul laid out in Romans 6.

THE PROPOSITION: JUST SAY NO TO SIN

Paul wasn't the type to pull punches when he taught the early Christian church. So his teaching on sin isn't hard to figure out. This is his basic proposition on the subject: *As Christians, we can and must say no to sin.* Paul set forth three crucial points in Romans 6 in this regard.

The first is this: *If we have trusted Christ as Savior and Lord, then we must embrace the fact that we have been identified with Christ's death and resurrection.* What does that mean for the believer every day? First, Jesus' death paid for our sin once for all, and so His death did away with its power over us. Second, Jesus' resurrection allows us to live life in a new way: free from the actions and attitudes of sin.

Paul described this incredible reality in Romans 6:6: "Knowing this, that our old self was crucified with Him, in order that our body of sin might be done away with, so that we would no longer be slaves to sin."

Throughout Romans 6 the dominant verb tenses are all in the past. That indicates something that God did once and for all in connection with sin through the cross of Christ. The point is simply this: The death and resurrection of Christ finally and completely dealt with sin. Look at what Paul said in verses 10–11: "For the death that He died, He died to sin once for all, but the life that He lives, He lives to God. Even so consider yourselves to be dead to sin, but alive to God in Christ Jesus."

Dead to Sin

Not long ago, I had a very moving experience as I spoke to about one hundred men at the Charlotte Rescue Mission in Charlotte, North Carolina. The director asked me to give a series of messages on the family and what it really means to be a husband and a father. It turned out to be one of the most gratifying, humbling, and moving experiences of my life.

You see, the hundred or so men who were there had all come from backgrounds of drug and alcohol abuse. They are all involved now in a Christ-centered rehabilitation program. Most of them had trusted Christ as Savior and Lord. I cannot tell you the sense of joy and the great privilege it was for me to spend time with these men, to hug them, and to see the tears in their eyes and the sense of hope that had been restored.

I was particularly moved by one testimony of a young man. "Kenny" told how his whole life had revolved around drugs and alcohol. He told how, as a preteen child, his father introduced him to alcohol. They became "drinking buddies." Then when he was just starting his teenage years, Kenny's mother introduced him to cocaine. In fact, they used to do drugs together. Kenny told how his life just plummeted from that point. Full of drugs and alcohol, he was controlled and addicted. But some years back, he was introduced to the program at the Charlotte Rescue Mission. He went to the program, and he gave his heart and life to Jesus Christ. And now he was returning to the mission to tell others his story. Before he came to Christ, he said, "I just couldn't help myself." He *had* to do drugs. He *had* to do alcohol, even though he hated himself for doing it. He was driven by his addictions.

"But now that I've given my life to Christ," Kenny said, "I have been set free. I know the joy of not having to do alcohol or drugs anymore." Like Kenny, you *can* say no to the attitudes and actions of sin. Romans 6:11 says you can: "Even so consider yourselves to be dead to sin, but alive to God in Christ Jesus."

Let's not kid ourselves. The fact that we have to continue to consider ourselves dead to sin shows that the possibility of sinning is ever present. But Paul said we have another option besides sin: *to continue to consider ourselves alive or constantly living for God.* Note the contrast. This is positive. We're dead to sin—its attitudes, actions, and power over us—but we are very much alive or living for Christ.

Alive to Christ Jesus

On October 17, 1998, at 6:42 P.M. I watched my mother breathe her last breath and walk into the arms of her Savior. Two weeks prior to that time, she had suffered a massive heart attack followed by a stroke. But before she had the stroke, as we visited her in the hospital, she kept saying to my two sisters and me, "I just want to be home. I just want to go see the Lord Jesus and see my husband."

It's not that Mom was giving up on life. She loved her children, grandchildren, and great-grandchildren to the very end. It was just that in the years since my dad's death —and in her own "fullness of years"—heaven became more of a joyful reality and expectancy for Mom. She loved the Lord Jesus more than she loved life itself. She wanted to be in His presence. That made her willing to go through the separation from the things in this world into the experience of everlasting, eternal life in the presence of the Savior that she had known and loved virtually all her life.

Jesus gave Mom the opportunity to experience life in a richer, fuller way even as she died. In much the same way, we can experience a fuller life because we can separate from the things of the world. Our sinful past has been cru cified. We're no longer obligated to live under the command of sin. When it raises its ugly head to tempt us, we must rely upon the historical reality that somehow, someway, we have been identified with Christ's death, burial, and resurrection. Therefore, sin no longer has the grip on us it once had. We are now free to walk out from under its power into the fullness of a righteous life.

I'm not denying that our sin is still very much alive and around us. But, thanks to Jesus Christ, we can count ourselves dead to sin and alive to God. To make that a reality, we need to encounter the second crucial point Paul offered about saying no to sin: *We must make a choice as to who and what we will serve.* Romans 6:12–14 makes the point this way:

> Therefore do not let sin reign in your mortal body so that you obey its lusts, and do not go on presenting the members of your body to sin as instruments of unrighteousness; but present yourselves to God as those alive from the dead, and your members as instruments of righteousness to God. For sin shall not be master over you, for you are not under law but under grace.

I believe that these three verses teach that we need to see all of life from a new perspective. They demand that anything that concerns us must not be given over to sin. Although sin may stick around as an outlaw, it should not be made a king. It should not be allowed to make laws, or oppress, or preside over the issues and affairs of our lives. It may live in the house, but it is not head of the household.

The expression "mortal body" here implies that the abuse of sin may show up in our physical bodies, *but we must not consent to that abuse.* Sinful acts confirm and strengthen sinful habits. One sin begets another. Sin is never satisfied until it completely destroys us. That's why we must not accommodate it but work on getting rid of it.

Sin is like a little bit of termite damage in a wood frame house. If you don't take care of that quickly and decisively, the whole house will come crumbling down. When sin raises its ugly head, we must make a choice not to wink at it, not to minimize it, but to deal with it decisively and quickly.

The third crucial point Paul offered in Romans 6 is *to keep ever before us our first and foremost allegiance to our Lord and Savior Jesus Christ*. Verse 16 says, "Do you not know that when you present yourselves to someone as slaves for obedience, you are slaves of the one whom you obey, either of sin resulting in death, or of obedience resulting in righteousness?"

The point is obvious: Whoever—or whatever—we follow controls us. To put it another way, we are slaves to the one to whom we hand ourselves over. If we hand ourselves over to sin, then the outcome is death. If we become slaves of obedience to God, the outcome is righteousness.

Handed Over to God

The process of "handing yourself over" is a constant affirmation of allegiance. At this writing, Karen and I have been married for nearly thirty years. We have a wonderful family, and we have a tremendous relationship. I regularly thank God for this wonderful gift that He has given to me in the person of my dear wife Karen. She is absolutely the joy of my life.

Through the years we have learned that one of the keys to a successful relationship is not just what you say, but it's what you do to feed and fuel the relationship. It takes time, commitment, and sacrifice to demonstrate and prove love for another person. But you know what? The more you demonstrate it, the more sacrifices you make, the easier it becomes. You develop depth and strength in the relationship. Your love is deeper and more vibrant as the years go by.

The constant yielding to each other builds strength and walls of protection around the relationship. However, paradoxically, unless there is that constant, continual work on the relationship, misplaced priorities and self-centeredness will ambush the relationship. We will become victims of our own sin.

Sin is like cancer. Cancer feeds off healthy cells. If the cancer is detected early, surgery and chemotherapy can destroy the cancer cells. Christ's death is God's radical surgery to remove the cancer of sin and its stain. Our yielding to God is God's chemotherapy to go after the residue. And that, in a way, is what the apostle Paul was speaking of in Romans 6. As we make the choice and decision continually, consistently, to yield ourselves as instruments of God's righteousness, to affirm that allegiance every day, the light of God's holiness burns away the sin that would seek to destroy us on a daily basis.

But a major challenge still remains: the daily battle against sin.

CHAPTER FOUR

Winning the Daily Battle Against Sin

Have you ever seen kudzu? I live in Georgia, and much of our state is covered with an out-of-control vine called "kudzu." Some people say kudzu came from the South Pacific. Others say it came from the fifth level of Dante's Inferno. But wherever it came from, it's almost impossible to kill. Kudzu is a hearty plant. It can grow up to nine inches a day. It chokes the life out of anything and everything in its path. And if kudzu ever finds its way to your property, it could take prayer and fasting to drive it out. I haven't seen much else work against it.

I have a friend who has waged an ongoing war against kudzu in his backyard. I went to his house one day to offer a sympathetic ear. He showed me where he'd first noticed the kudzu in his yard. He recounted his battle against the pernicious vine. He shook his head—still in disbelief that the kudzu refused to surrender to his best efforts against it—as he told me, "You know, Crawford, no matter what I do, that kudzu keeps coming back! I chop at it. I work on it. I pull it up. And every time it comes back, and it comes back with a vengeance, brother!"

The daily battle against sin is very much like the daily battle against kudzu. In this chapter, we'll look into both the *problem* of sin and the *prescription* for victory in our daily battle against it.

I'M NOT OK, AND I'M
PRETTY SURE YOU AREN'T EITHER

You remember those glorious teenage years, when you felt invincible and let the whole world know it somehow? "Andrew," a teenage son of one of my good friends, let his dad know he thought he would be invincible against temptation not long ago. The event was classic for us parents: Andrew wanted to attend a party that his father felt would take him to the limits of his willpower. His dad remembered what such parties had done for his own spiritual life in high school. As a consequence, he said no to Andrew.

"Dad, you've always trusted me!" Andrew was hurt by his father's refusal to give the permission he sought. "Why won't you trust me this time?"

My friend offered this bit of wisdom. "Because after all you've told me," he said, "I feel uncomfortable with who you said was going to be there. I'm not comfortable with what you said would go on at that party. Technically, it's not true that I don't trust you, Son. But I don't trust your flesh. Neither do I trust my own."

My friend certainly understood the problem with sin: *The problem with sin is that no one—and I mean no one—escapes it.* Andrew wanted to do good. His father wanted to do good too. The "want-to" to do what was right was never at question. The problem was what Paul the apostle laid out in Romans 7:21: "I find then the principle that evil is present in me."

Just when you think you've dealt with the problem of sin, just like kudzu you find it growing in your spiritual backyard again. We've already said that sin can be beaten through Jesus Christ. But the process of rooting it out in everyday life is a genuine struggle that Paul covered in Romans 7. It's a battle between two natures: the old nature and the new nature. Paul spelled it out like this: "For the good that I want, I do not do, but I practice the very evil that I do not want. But if I am doing the very thing I do not want, I am no longer the one doing it, but sin which dwells in me" (Romans 7:19–20).

Two Warriors

There are two I's in this section. The first "I" is the old nature, which asserts its rights. The new nature wants to do what is right, but the old nature goes ahead and does what it wants to. Paul showed us how to deal with sin in Romans 6, yet the most acute problem of all still remains: the evil that is present in us. That is the evil that causes me to respond in rebellion when I encounter God's righteous standards. Those standards are all right, but I am all wrong!

Karen and I have friends with a teenage daughter who has jumped headfirst into rebellion. One day over lunch they told us their struggle with her. In exasperation the girl's father said to us, "You know, Crawford and Karen, it seems that whatever we tell her to do, she willfully does the exact opposite."

My first reaction was to think, *Boy, that's terrible! How could she be that way?* My next reaction was to think, *That sounds just like me.*

You see, there's a side of me—and of you—that is strangely drawn toward doing the very opposite of what God says we should do. Paul struggled with the same issue. What was the apostle's solution? We need to note that his response was not to reject God's standards. Instead, Paul's response was to focus on his inability to keep those standards. He made this clear in Romans 7:13–14:

Therefore did that which is good [God's righteous standards expressed through His law and commands] become a cause of death for me? May it never be! Rather it was sin, in order that it might be shown to be sin by effecting my death through that which is good, so that through the commandment sin would become utterly sinful. For we know that the Law is spiritual, but I am of flesh, sold into bondage to sin.

Paul said that part of our problem is this: Because we are sinners, we do not readily believe or accept sin for what it really is. That's why God uses the Law to show us clearly what sin is—and what it intends to do. There's no confusion in the apostle about the line between right and wrong. But in Romans 7:15, Paul admitted to some confusion within him: "For what I am doing, I do not understand."

This is a statement of a man who is baffled. Paul just didn't understand why he naturally withdraws from doing the right thing. I must confess that I don't understand that about myself, either. For the most part, neither do you.

Every last one of us can identify with the apostle Paul here. For we, too, know what it means to be under the domination of sin. Our battle is not a few isolated conflicts, but a continual warfare. The conflict arises because we want to serve God, but we find ourselves compellingly drawn toward serving self and sin. Like Paul, it is not our true self that does the evil, but the sin that dwells in us. Sin causes us to forget who we are in Christ.

My children can drive themselves to school these days. (A couple of them, in fact, are driving themselves to work and their own homes.) But before they could drive themselves, I took them to school every day. We'd have prayer in our car on the way to school. One of the last things I would say as they got out of the car was, "Remember who you are today."

I wasn't talking about the possibility that they'd forget their names and addresses. They knew exactly what I was saying: Their identities and values as Christians, as followers of Jesus Christ, and as members of the Loritts household should affect their behavior that particular day. Whenever they didn't live up to who they are, it was not because they didn't want to. It was just that they were drawn toward something that was more compelling at the moment. Whenever they failed, their true selves in Jesus Christ did not have mastery over them.

My children were reminded of a crucial lesson each day with the encouragement to remember who they are. *Apart from who we are in Christ, we should never trust ourselves.* Our flesh and natural inclinations are powerful. They will always lead in the wrong direction. Paul reminded us graphically in Romans 7:18 that we can't afford to put our confidence in the flesh: "For I know that nothing good dwells in me, that is, in my flesh; for the willing is present in me, but the doing of the good is not."

The Power of Temptation

The absence of good in the flesh is another way of saying that oil and water do not mix. Where the flesh is powerful, the will to do good becomes powerless.

In a letter he wrote in the year before his death, Benjamin Franklin made the now-famous quote, "In this world nothing can be said to be certain, except death and taxes." Franklin was probably being philosophical as he faced the end of his own life. So much for the "death" part, then. But the part about taxes still drives many of us to grief.

My friend Phil is no exception. Phil is a phenomenal businessman. Like many others in the business community, Phil has taken advantage of every possible legal means to avoid paying more than his share of taxes. He still ends up paying a substantial amount each year.

Phil is active in a local Christian businessmen's group. He understands from personal experience how painful it can be for a small businessman to write a check for payroll or income taxes that all but wipes out the checking ac-

count. Yet he took his faith—and his role as a leader in that
group—seriously enough that he not only kept writing
those checks, but kept reminding others in the group that
they should, too. "Pay the dollar; save your honor" was his
constant reminder.

For years and years, Phil kept those taxes paid in full
without a second thought. But in a time of recession a few
years ago, Phil was losing faith that his business would survive into the next quarter. When April of that year rolled
around, and it was time to make good for both quarterly
payroll taxes *and* his annual income taxes, Phil came face-
to-face with a harsh reality. He realized the checks he
would write that month would put his bank balances—
savings and checking alike—as close to the zero figure as
he'd been since his first year in business.

Phil simmered at the thought. He'd been working all
these years, and the government was about to take him
back to ground zero. He knew forty different tricks he
could use in "gray areas" to keep some money in his accounts. He'd never used them before. He always believed it
was honoring to God to avoid even a hint of impropriety in
his bookkeeping. Yet he knew that other businessmen put
them into play all the time. Maybe it was time now to tell
his accountant to do the same.

But before he took that action, he asked two of his closest friends from his businessmen's fellowship to meet him
for coffee. "Fellows, I need some wisdom. You know I've
been at everyone else in the group to be above reproach in
taxpaying and keeping books. You know I've been the one
among us that says, 'Pay the dollar; save your honor.'
Maybe it's been too easy for me to say that.

"Right now, I'm thinking about letting my accountant
keep my books more like everyone else. If I write the
checks I'd write according to the rules I've been using, my
cash flow will be as good as gone. I have no way of knowing if business will pick up with enough volume to meet

next month's payroll. But if I go ahead and do some 'gray accounting' like almost everyone else I know, I'm halfway to meeting next month's expenses.

"So you tell me: *Was I being too idealistic about how I keep my books?*"

To Phil's surprise, tears began to well up in his friend Harry's eyes. "Phil…" Harry stammered as he began staring at the table. "Phil, I always thought you were a little nuts to be so conscientious about paying the government every possible cent you could. But last year, I got to thinking you probably slept better at night than I did. And that you probably never worried about being audited like I did. And that your way of business was probably way more honoring to God than mine.

"Phil, you finally got to me. I've ordered my accountant to keep my books like you've always said I should . . . *and now you're thinking about backing out of doing the right thing?* Hey, I can loan you the money to keep going for a while at no interest if that's what it takes. But now—after all these years—don't give in to less than what you know is best. Please."

That was all Phil needed to hear. He kept his books and paid his taxes as he always had. Just as he'd figured, his accounts were nearly wiped out that April. For a few months, Phil's business was touch and go. But he never had to take Harry up on the loan offer—and his business finally recovered.

Paying taxes is one of those areas where it can be tough to keep your integrity. But remember when you're tempted to cheat that your integrity matters not only to you, but to those who are watching you. And, believe me, there are usually more people watching you than you ever dreamed possible.

Overpowering Forces

Sin keeps after us, doesn't it? It's relentless in its pursuit of us. Perhaps as you're reading these words you've become acutely aware once again of the areas in which you struggle. Maybe you have painful memories of the sins that have beaten you down. You desperately want to do what's right, but you find yourself asking, "How come it's taking so long for me to get better?" Like the apostle Paul, you're not rebelling or fighting God's Law or what He has said. You joyfully want to do that. You agree with Paul in Romans 7:22, "For I joyfully concur with the law of God in the inner man."

The expression "inner man" refers to a person's "heart of hearts." Here, Paul said his inner man reflects his new nature in Jesus Christ. That new nature desires to please God. But Paul openly acknowledged that the power of sin kept pulling him away from what he wanted to do in his heart of hearts. Romans 7:23 says, "But I see a different law in the members of my body, waging war against the law of my mind and making me a prisoner of the law of sin which is in my members."

In January 1999, I was stranded in San Francisco. I couldn't get a flight back to my home in Atlanta, no matter how much I wanted one. The problem was bad weather. Ice and terrible snowstorms in the Midwest and Southeast had cancelled flights in those regions of the country. The domino effect from those stranded planes had reached the West Coast.

I had been away from home for a while. I wanted desperately to see my family and to sleep in my own bed, instead of looking forward to a fitful sleep in the San Francisco airport lounge waiting for circumstances to change. Do you know something? All the "want-to" in the world that day didn't make one bit of difference in getting me home. My wants that day just didn't matter. My desire to be home was overruled by forces over which I had no control.

In much the same way, the forces of sin are beyond my personal control. In our own strength, our desire to do what is right will not change what is wrong with us. It's exactly as Paul put it in Romans 7:24: "Wretched man that I am! Who will set me free from the body of this death?"

"The body of this death" is the scene of this contest. It's the battleground for the struggle. Sin living in the members of our own bodies brings spiritual death to us. We become aware that we need outside help—that without it, we'll be stuck forever in the frustration of a spiritual airport that will take us nowhere.

Take note that Paul wasn't asking to be delivered from his body as such. He was asking to be delivered from the spiritual death that characterizes the body. In other words, Paul pled for freedom from his own evil actions that opposed his desire to do that which is good.

Paul compared the pervasive sin nature to a dead body, which according to Jewish ceremonial law was unlawful and defiling to touch. Paul used this despicable illustration to alert everyone to the horrible nature of sin: For the Christian, the body of sin is like carrying about a decaying corpse every day of our lives.

Paul's desire was for every Christian to see how desperate we are in our inability to get rid of this corpse. We are truly in need of Someone to set us free from the rotting cadaver that sin becomes for each of us. The apostle wanted to trigger a sickening disgust of sin in us—and a passion to do anything to get rid of it.

If we were to leave our struggle against sin at this stage of the process, we'd be left with a dismaying problem. But we don't leave the struggle here—not at all. Instead, we have a source of practical righteousness with which to engage the battle. If we let it, it empowers our motives and conduct in daily living. God does not leave us in despair. Through Christ, we can indeed be liberated from the tyranny of sin that dwells within us. Jesus offers the ultimate solution for our everyday struggle with sin—and the victorious prescription of how to win that battle.

DAILY HORSEPOWER TO WIN THE BATTLE

Over the years I've had the privilege of hearing many gifted Bible teachers. I have enjoyed being in the congregations of many godly pastors. I am constantly honored to see the way God works through these leaders to achieve His ends.

Yet many of my personal heroes are the men and women who quietly live their lives as overcomers of sin and its power. Some are public figures. Most are not. But they all share this common characteristic: the daily "horsepower" to win the battle against sin.

How much is enough? Allen Redpath, a great Bible teacher, was fond of telling the story of a wealthy gentleman who bought a Rolls Royce. The man went to the dealer to examine the car. He took it for a test drive, and he was satisfied with its overall performance. In fact, he had never driven anything like it in his life. The vehicle was living up to the brand's reputation as the ultimate in automobiles.

Just as he was about ready to give the salesman the check for the car, it dawned on him that he hadn't asked about the car's horsepower. For some strange reason, the gentleman insisted that the salesman tell him the car's horsepower before he handed over the check. The salesman was surprised. The buyer had already taken it for a test drive, and he had found the car to his liking. Why the need for more details? The salesman replied, "Sir, I don't have the details about this. I'll get them for you as soon as I can." The salesman wired the home office with the question.

By return telegram came this two-word message: "Horsepower adequate."

We're about to launch into the solution for your daily battle against sin. Paul outlined a marvelous prescription in Romans 8 that is God's "Rolls Royce" method to win your battle against sin each day. The horsepower here is more than adequate to overcome sin—and isn't that what we came for in the first place? God's power source is none other than the third person of the Trinity Himself, the Holy Spirit.

You don't need to bandy about the details, then. You need to put God's prescription against sin into action.

The heart of Romans 8 could be summed up in this simple statement: *We have been set free from the power of sin by the Spirit of God.* Paul's simple—and revolutionary—statement of Romans 8:2 says, "For the law of the Spirit of life in Christ Jesus has set you free from the law of sin and of death."

Paul put the law of the spirit of life in Christ Jesus in direct contrast to the law of sin and death. These laws constantly influence the actions we take in everyday life. The good news for believers in Jesus Christ is this: Because the Spirit of God is living inside of us, Christians are not helpless in our battle against sin.

The Law of Moses was certainly set against sin, yet it prescribed a way of life that those of us in the flesh could not follow. Only the Spirit of God in us could release the power we need to overcome the seemingly irresistible temptation to fall to sin. All of the righteous requirements of God are met in our daily lives as we yield ourselves to the controlling power of His Spirit who lives within us.

Our flesh can still be a seat of rebellion in each of us. This rebellion produces a way of thinking and a pattern of behavior. Likewise, the Holy Spirit produces a way of thinking and a certain pattern of behavior. Paul laid this out simply in Romans 8:5–6: "For those who are according to the flesh set their minds on the things of the flesh, but those who are according to the Spirit, the things of the Spirit. For the mind set on the flesh is death, but the mind set on the Spirit is life and peace."

The direction and outlook of the mind can make a life-and-death difference. If your mind is set on the flesh, Paul said it's the equivalent of "spiritual death." "Life and peace" is the product of the mind set on the Spirit of God. The point here is that yieldedness and obedience to the presence of God's Spirit in our lives conquers the sin that is around us and in us.

OFFERING CONTROL

We're not just talking about "positive thinking" here. It's far deeper than that. We're talking about our minds focusing on the resident person of the Holy Spirit, and then allowing Him to fill our thoughts and to trigger the reaction of our wills to do the right thing.

This demands a conscious decision on our part. You see, the Spirit of God will never violate our wills. In order to engage and appropriate His power, we must actively and obediently yield to His presence. Failure to yield to His presence means, of necessity, that we cave in to the presence of sin that is within us.

That being said, *we do not have to cave in to the presence and principle of sin.* Look at what Paul said in Romans 8:11: "But if the Spirit of Him who raised Jesus from the dead dwells in you, He who raised Christ Jesus from the dead will also give life to your mortal bodies through His Spirit who dwells in you."

I'm beside myself with this thought! The same power that raised Jesus from the dead resides in us every day of our lives! All we must do is yield to that power, and He conquers sin and death—every day and forever—*in us!* In these "mortal bodies" (as Paul put it) resides the third person of the Godhead, to strengthen us, to aid us, to give us all that we need. He doesn't leave us. He doesn't forsake us. He is there for us to receive our obedience. He is there to direct our footsteps and to lead us into victory.

As in chapter 6 of Romans, however, the apostle Paul reminded us here in chapter 8 that we hold the choice to offer control of our lives to the Spirit of God. Again, God will not violate our wills; He won't suddenly rush in and block our willful choices. We must willfully choose to yield to His will and to His presence in our lives. Paul underscored this principle in verses 12 and 13 when he said, "So then, brethren, we are under obligation, not to the flesh, to live according to the flesh—for if you are living according to the flesh, you must die; but if by the Spirit you are putting to death the deeds of the body, you will live."

Notice here that "putting to death the deeds of the body" is a progressive, continual dependence upon the Spirit of God. Paul indicated that this is not a "once and for all" experience with God's Spirit, but an ongoing reliance upon His Spirit every day of our lives.

This suggests that the sin nature is never done away with this side of heaven. It is always there. That's why we must continuously rely upon the presence of the Spirit of God to work in us and through us in overcoming sin.

Note that Romans 8:12–13 also teaches that we are not in debt to the flesh as if we are obliged to do its bidding. Do you know what that means? *We do not have to sin.* Instead, this passage strongly implies that we are debtors to Christ and to the Holy Spirit. Through the death of our wonderful Savior on the cross in our place and for our sins, we have been delivered from the penalty of sin. Right now, during our pilgrimage this side of heaven, we're being delivered from the power of sin over our lives as we yield ourselves to the Spirit of God.

God has given us everything that we need to be victorious over sin. In that sense, we have an obligation to be obedient followers and to plug into the "power source" that He has so graciously given to us. Being delivered from so great a death by so great a ransom, we are deeply indebted to our deliverer, the Lord Jesus.

I tell you that God, through the power of the Spirit, is able not only to empower us right now but also to take all the sinful mess and debris that has built up in our lives. He will cleanse us. He can make us flourish once again.

The Yellowstone National Park fire of 1988 was noted for its massive devastation. But naturalists also made note of a certain strain of jack pine that emerged shortly after the fire. The seeds of this pine cannot be released from the cone unless put under intense heat. Yet these young trees were defining the new life springing out of the ashes of Yellowstone.

The refining fire of God can bring new life to us too. Seeds of righteousness can be released and flourish where once there was only the dead, decaying wood of rebellion. If we yield in obedience to the Spirit of God, new life can spring forth where only sin could previously be seen.

The choice is ours.

CHAPTER FIVE

The Divine Distance

I have two older sisters. One is four years older than I am, and the other is three years older than I am. When we were kids, we sometimes played house. My sisters dressed up like my mother. Of course, I played the role of my father. I wanted to walk like him, talk like him, and just generally act like him. In retrospect, it's no wonder why: I've always admired my dad. In fact, next to Jesus Christ, he's the greatest influence in my life.

I wanted to reflect the character of my dad whenever I could. I truly wanted to look like him not only during playtime with my sisters, but all along the way as I grew into manhood. As Christians, we have a distinct responsibility and an awesome opportunity: to reflect the holiness of God. The apostle Peter reminded the early church of this in 1 Peter 1:13–16:

> Therefore, prepare your minds for action, keep sober in spirit, fix your hope completely on the grace to be brought to you at the revelation of Jesus Christ. As obedient children, do not be conformed to the former lusts

which were yours in your ignorance, but like the Holy One who called you, be holy yourselves also in all your behavior; because it is written, "You shall be holy, for I am holy."

In these words, God sets the standard for authentic Christianity. He points to the direction and outcome of genuine Christianity in the context of a fallen world. It is the expression and demonstration and display of nothing less than His holiness.

Holiness, then, is a crucial part of "making it home" for a Christian. So now the critical question is, What does it mean to be holy?

THE HOLINESS OF GOD

To start, our call to holiness means we should reflect the character of God to whom we are related. And so the question is, Whom do we look like?

Just as I wanted to look like my dad as his son, I desire to look like God as His child. Yet I never exactly captured Dad's mannerisms and character. Nor will I exactly capture God's holiness this side of heaven. At best our holiness is a relative thing. No matter how close we come to an accurate reflection of God's holiness, we're still so very far away.

In fact, the very word *holiness* denotes the awesome, incredible distance and distinction between God, our Creator, and us, His creatures. When we embrace this paradox, oddly enough, that's when we are closest to the heart of God. The Bible teaches this clearly. Look at these words in Isaiah 57:15: "For thus says the high and exalted One who lives forever, whose name is Holy, 'I dwell on a high and holy place, and also with the contrite and lowly of spirit in order to revive the spirit of the lowly and to revive the heart of the contrite.'"

This is a call to embrace the divine distance between ourselves and our holy heavenly Father. The true candidates to "make it home" through spiritual revival and renewal are those who are contrite and lowly of spirit. Those who may expect help from God are those who sense their own distance from God and His holiness. These are the people who grasp the difference between *God's place* and *our position.*

God Himself declares, "I dwell on a high and holy place." The point is this: God says these things in order to keep our relationship in perspective. God wants all of humanity to know His "address" as the Sovereign of the universe in contrast to their "address" as fallen creatures.

God is exalted infinitely above every creature. In fact, God is exalted beyond anything we can conceive about Him. There is no creature like the Creator, of course. God is both immortal and immutable. We are neither. Our reflection of God's holiness, then, has to begin with recognizing God's place in the universe. In the words of Matthew Henry, "Whoever has business with God must go to Him as our Father in heaven, because that is where He dwells."

Yet I am haunted by the feeling that we have lost our awe of God. On more than one occasion, I have been in church services where the entire emphasis has been on how we feel about God and what we need Him to do for us. Don't get me wrong; I believe God is committed to meeting all of our needs. God loves us infinitely. He does care about our hearts' desires and our feelings toward Him. But there has been a shift in our worship in recent years, I think, in which we place a greater emphasis on who we are rather than the greatness of God. In short, much of the church and modern Christianity has lost the awe and the fear of God in our pursuit for relevance and having our own "needs" met. In so doing, we have reduced God to the level of our humanity.

We run the risk of domesticating God. I sometimes sense that we treat God as if He were the family pet that exists solely for our comfort and enjoyment. In this regard, we have been inordinately influenced by our culture. It's as if we celebrate a God who assists us, but who would never say that we are wrong or that our desires sometimes are sinful. The atmosphere seems to be permeated with the need for affirmation as our highest priority.

That leads to the rejection of a God who would say that we are not OK, much less demand that we change our behavior to His standards of holiness. We are more than willing to talk or sing about God's love, but as soon as the conversation, the sermon, or the hymn turns to God's holiness and our accountability to Him, we tune out or change the subject.

This is another glaring indication of widespread confusion concerning God's love and grace. God's love and grace do not embrace sin. God cannot accommodate sin. The death of our Savior has resolved the issue of sin, as we saw in the last two chapters. However, we need to be constantly reminded of the words of Paul in Romans 6:1–2: "What shall we say then? Are we to continue in sin so that grace may increase? May it never be! How shall we who died to sin still live in it?"

Paul brought the same issue to light in 2 Corinthians 5:15: "And He died for all, so that they who live might no longer live for themselves, but for Him who died and rose again on their behalf."

God's love and grace are not excuses to continue in sinful self-centered behavior. No! His love and grace should drive us and motivate us to please Him and to passionately pursue His holiness. And that is precisely the point of 2 Corinthians 5:9: "Therefore we also have as our ambition, whether at home or absent, to be pleasing to Him." Anything less than this intentional pursuit is, in the words of Dietrich Bonhoeffer, "cheap grace."

I know a pastor who committed adultery—repeatedly and blatantly. He justified it by saying that each time he had sex with the other woman, he confessed his sin to the Lord and God forgave him. He soothed his seared conscience by convincing himself that because God is such a loving and forgiving God, his sinful activity would not be held against him. What's more, his ministry grew as he engaged in adultery. He was preaching with more "power" and results than ever before. According to his spiritually demented thinking, greater results were certainly evidence that everything was just fine. However, not long ago this very deception destroyed him. His sin was uncovered. His ministry and family are gone. And, as of this writing, he has yet to repent.

Our mind games and moral smoke and mirrors in the end fool no one but ourselves. I cannot say this strongly enough: *God does not play with sin.* In the words of my dear friend Tim Cash, you cannot experience holiness without practicing obedience. In like manner, it follows that there cannot be forgiveness without true repentance.

The key to embracing repentance as an identity and lifestyle is lodged in our concept of God. More specifically, an understanding and an appreciation of the holiness of God will draw us to His heart and character—and away from ourselves and our sin.

Whom do we look like? A domesticated God formed after our own image—or the holy Sovereign who dwells on a high and holy place?

EVERYDAY HOLINESS

Biblically, to be holy is to be morally blameless. It means to be separated from sin and consecrated to God. So to live a holy life means to live a life that conforms to God's moral precepts, in contrast to the sinful ways of the world and the culture in which we live.

Yet experiencing God's holiness is the challenge of the Christian life. One of the primary reasons we do not experience more holiness in our daily living is because, in the words of Jerry Bridges, our attitude toward sin is more self-centered than God-centered. It's a matter of focus. We can be more concerned about our "victory over sin" than we are about the fact that our sins grieve the heart of God. It seems ironic, but in these cases we see sin as a block to our personal success more than an offense to God.

As a result, we can make holiness a measurement of our spiritual success rather than a reflection of the God who defines it through His distinct differences from us. We begin to think that we can make holiness our possession on a whim rather than pursuing a lifetime discipline of obedience. Just like the pastor I mentioned, we sometimes deceive ourselves when we play with temptation by entertaining the thought that if we sin we can always confess it and ask for forgiveness later.

This thinking is always dangerous. God never overlooks our sin. He does not decide to brush it aside because the sin is a "small one." No, God hates sin intensely. It doesn't matter how big or small it is in our reckoning. It doesn't matter where or when God finds it. God is in the most complete sense separated from all evil. It is impossible for Him to sin—and it seems impossible for us *not* to sin this side of heaven.

A Reflection, Not a Possession

So what does the Bible mean when it calls for us to be holy? Let's take a closer look at God's holiness as it is reflected in humanity:

- First, our holiness is an outcome of God's saving work.

- Second, the holiness required of mankind in the Scriptures has to do with character and conduct.

- Third, in many cases the holiness given to mankind in the Scriptures has to do with God's calling, assignments to be accomplished, and the dedication of those assignments to God's purposes.

• Finally, we can and must grow in holiness in this life.

To avoid being totally frustrated, we have to have a realistic perception of the discipline holiness requires. Holiness is not an "instant achievement." Consider Paul's encouragement in 2 Corinthians 7:1: "Therefore, having these promises, beloved, let us cleanse ourselves from all defilement of flesh and spirit, perfecting holiness in the fear of God."

Paul was describing a process of daily choices. Our part is to cooperate with God's ongoing transformation of our hearts regarding sin and righteousness. Only then will we be able to fulfill the destiny described in 1 Thessalonians 3:13: "So that He may establish your hearts without blame in holiness before our God and Father at the coming of our Lord Jesus with all His saints."

What all this means is that we cannot resemble God in His perfection and attributes by our own efforts. We can, however, *reflect* His likeness when we show righteousness in character and conduct, and when we display the love in which true holiness demonstrates itself.

In order to *reflect* God's likeness, we must *respect* His position. This is the "divine distance" we have to recognize. We are not God. Without His grace through Jesus Christ, there is an insurmountable gap between the holy God and even His children.

It's not unlike earthly parents and their children. Some time ago, one of our children crossed the Respect Line with me. That child was just getting too familiar with me in response to a question I'd asked.

I believe my children would be the first to tell you that I don't carry myself as some egomaniac promenading around my house demanding that my wife and children bow in worship of me. (At least I hope they would.) However, there *is* an appropriate distance that parents must keep with regard to their children. This "distance" helps main-

tain the proper amount of respect for a parent and to en-
sure character development in the child's life.

That's why I asked three questions when my child
crossed the Respect Line with me. First I turned, looked
that child in the eye, and said, "I need to ask you to think
with me: To whom are you talking?" My child answered
with the obvious, "You."

Secondly I asked, "Who am I?" My child's response
was, "You're my father."

That's when I knew we were getting somewhere. I was
able to ask the third question: "Who are you then?"

The answer: "Well, I'm your child." Then the lights
went on. The child wasn't the parent. In fact, the child was
nowhere close to my role—and recognized it.

I sometimes wonder if God doesn't sit on His throne in
heaven and respond to us in much the same way when *we*
cross the Respect Line. As we get "overly familiar" with
God, I wonder if He says to us, "To whom are you talking?
Do you understand who I am? Do you know who you are?"

We like to exalt our needs rather than embrace our
neediness. We want a God who will serve us and be what
we want Him to be, rather than a God who expects us to
bow and surrender in brokenness in the presence of His
holiness. *Only the latter posture makes us candidates for His
divine compassion and grace.*

God's "divine distance" ought to inspire us with a holy
reverence of Him. It should create in us a supreme confidence and faith in Him. God's holiness should only magnify
His compassion to us. Just think: He who rides in the heav-
ens stoops to concern Himself with us! An appreciation of
the profound holiness of God should strike in our hearts an
awesome sense of respect and a desire to defer to His will.

Humility and Contrition

On October 17, 1998, my mother went home to be
with the Lord. Several years ago, my mother had asked me

if I would preach her funeral when that time came. Before I realized what I had committed myself to, I responded by saying yes, and so I did. I preached her funeral not because I was some emotional hero, but because she asked me to do it. In fact, because of my mother's godliness, great humility and commitment to her family, and the years of sacrifice that she had made on our behalf, frankly, I would have done anything she had asked me to do.

Mom was a prime example that God lives "with the contrite and lowly." And this ought to be our position. The word *contrite* means the active remembrance of the pain and the sorrow that our sin has caused. God has tender compassion on the contrite, and on those who are aware of their sinfulness and come into His presence broken and without excuses.

I have a friend who is a Christian and a professional athlete. He has struggled for a number of years with sexual temptation. He was caught propositioning a prostitute. Of course, it made the news. The papers and the electronic media gave it a lot of play and publicity.

What I have been most impressed with has been his genuine repentance. Despite the terrible sin, despite the shame on himself, his family, and his friends, my friend will make no excuses for himself. He completely owns up to the fact that his actions were wrong. He is getting help and is being restored as of this writing. My heart is deeply touched with his genuine desire to overcome the sin in his life and to own up to his responsibilities. He is truly contrite.

People who are contrite realize that, but for the grace of God, at any moment the bottom can fall out of their lives. They are the people who feel the shame and rejection of others and who carry the embarrassment of their failure or who realize how close all of us are to sin and shame. It is with these people that God lives! He visits them graciously; He talks with them as a familiar Friend by His Word and through His Spirit as we would talk to our own family.

God lives in the lowest heart. He inhabits sincerity as surely as He inhabits eternity. He revives and renews the contrite heart and spirit. He gives life and wholeness to broken, defeated, and fearful hearts. This renewed life from God Himself is sufficient to counterbalance all of the griefs and failures and fears that break and conquer our lives. His presence drives away sin and brings revival.

The holiness of God is not an abstract reality. It is a practical blessing. It is to be demonstrated every day of our lives. Jerry Bridges says in his book *The Pursuit of Holiness,* "The pursuit of holiness is a joint venture between God and the Christian. No one can attain any degree of holiness without God working in his life, but just as surely no one will attain it without effort on his own part. God has made it possible for us to walk in holiness but he has given us the responsibility of doing the walking."[1]

That is precisely the point of the apostle Paul's statement in Philippians 2:12–13: "So then, my beloved, just as you have always obeyed, not as in my presence only, but now much more in my absence, work out your salvation with fear and trembling; for it is God who is at work in you, both to will and to work for His good pleasure."

The presence of a holy God in our lives should drive us to pursue holiness—and to work on those areas in our lives that don't conform to His image.

Some years ago my wife brought home an ugly green desk. It was awful. I thought the best thing we could do for it was to take an axe to it and throw it out. But Karen saw something that our children and I didn't see. Right from the start Karen said, "I'm going to refinish this thing. You watch what happens."

So the next few days she scraped and stripped the layers of paint off the desk. Karen sanded and sanded some more, and—to our amazement—underneath all of that mess was a beautiful oak desk. It sits in our family room to this very day.

Holiness demands diligent attention to the mess in our lives. In this regard, repentance is a foundational response to God's holiness. The contrasting stories of David and Joseph and their battles with temptation underscore this point.

David fell into adultery with Bathsheba not only because he was in the wrong place, but literally because his eyes were on the wrong thing: a beautiful woman who was another man's wife taking a bath. He lost sight of the holiness of his loving, gracious God. When he lowered his sights, he lost desire to please God.

Joseph, on the other hand, overcame the seemingly irresistible temptation of a woman wishing to seduce him because he remembered the love and favor God had showered on him. Most important, he had a deep appreciation of and kept his sights on the holiness of God. Thus he looked sin in the eye and said, "How then could I do this great evil and sin against God?" (Genesis 39:9).

The holiness of God requires us to turn from our sin toward Him. In a word, we need to repent.

But where and how do we do that?

NOTE

1. Jerry Bridges, *The Pursuit of Holiness* (Colorado Springs: NavPress, 1978), 14.

CHAPTER SIX

A Place
to Repent

Some friends of mine who are Christian musicians tell of a time they were scheduled to play a concert in Michigan in the dead of winter. An ice storm had swept through the area several days before, and its effects were still being felt. The building that hosted the concert was way out in the country—one of several sites for a huge denominational youth event.

My friends drove for hours over ice-covered roads to make it to the venue. They pulled up to the building later than they had hoped. Once there, they found volunteers ready to unload their van. They were grateful for the help, of course, as they scrambled to set up.

The promoters of the event had arranged for that help because they needed to use my friends' van to help transport the youth from the various seminar locations of the convention to the central concert location. Once they checked to make sure all their concert gear was unloaded, my friends were happy to help out. They surrendered their keys to one of the promoters, and then they grabbed their luggage to change into their concert clothing.

The problem was, there was nowhere in the building to change. The harsh cold had frozen the pipes in the building, and the bathrooms were sealed off. There were portable facilities there, but not much else. Kids were streaming into the building as church vans and buses brought them in. Because the musicians' own van was part of that effort, they didn't even have the option to change for the concert in there.

They did the concert in the clothing they'd traveled in for twelve hours that day. They couldn't even splash water on their faces before they started. "Go figure," one friend told me later with a grin. "We spent a typical night encouraging kids to change, but *we* couldn't."

There was no physical room for my friends to change their clothing that night. But there was plenty of room for young people to repent and change at the end of that concert—and that's the most important kind of room the church needs to offer, isn't it?

WHERE DO YOU GO TO CHANGE?

I think one of the major barriers to people repenting is simply the fact that they cannot find a *place* to repent. Sometimes it's because people don't want to find that place. Other times it's because the church doesn't offer that place.

As of this writing, media are discussing a very prominent church leader whose sinful arrogance and corruption are causing his demise. Even more regrettable, his denomination has covered for him. By default, it has affirmed him in his sinfulness. Its actions were couched in the name of love, grace, and forgiveness. Yet grace never ignores or rejects the standards of holiness.

Grace is not hostile or punitive. Still, it affirms God's way of dealing with sin. It points to His gracious, lavish provision for our sin—the sacrifice of His dear Son for us on the cross. Grace should also point to the human response to sin: repentance.

In the case of the church leader just mentioned, grace never had a chance to have its proper impact. His sin was not dealt with and forsaken; it was simply glossed over. The church body surrounding him denied him a place to repent just as surely as other church bodies deny a place to repent due to their self-righteousness. Ironically, the law dealt with him when the church wouldn't.

This delicate balance between being lax about sin and being unforgiving raises a serious set of questions. What should our attitude be toward our brothers and sisters who are overcome by sin? How should we respond to them? What should we do when their sin is discovered? We have often fumbled the ball when dealing with sin in another person's life. We wrestle with who is responsible for approaching the person. We wonder how the person should be approached. We question the limitation of our confrontation.

I believe the answers to these concerns are found in three very important biblical mandates:

- The Christian community is required to be a place to repent (Hebrews 12:14–17).

- The Christian community is required to intentionally and directly address and confront sin (Matthew 18:15–17).

- The Christian community is required to have a right attitude in restoring repentant brothers and sisters (Galatians 6:1).

We'll unpack these mandates in this chapter and the two that follow.

In the Bible, repentance makes demands on both the sinner and the church. The sinner must change, and the church must restore the sinner into fellowship and spiritual health. Having said that, I know many of us hold different ideas about what restoration means, especially for those engaged in public ministry. Do we treat a local Sunday school teacher in the same way we treat the head of a denomination? Does "full restoration" mean the same thing for both individuals?

There can—and must—be complete spiritual restoration when a person repents and turns from sin. At the same time, I believe consequences to sin can permanently affect how broad-based one's ministry and influence can be in the future. But I do not believe, for example, that a pastor who falls into sin should be forever banished from the public pastoral ministry.

I believe the practical question of restoration surrounds the depth and sincerity of repentance. Repentance is proven by one's readiness to submit to godly discipline, which will include a series of benchmarks in the restoration process. Finally, one's restoration should be affirmed by godly leadership, who make it known when the process is over. The repentant person can't decide prematurely and on on his own initiative to go back into ministry.

An evangelist and pastor said that a person is qualified to be fully restored when the repentance concerning the sin is as broadly known as the sin that was originally committed. Indeed, both the repentant person and the church have serious responsibilities in the process of repentance.

BECOMING A PLACE TO REPENT

The Christian community is required to be a place to repent. Hebrews 12:14–17 states it plainly:

> Pursue peace with all men, and the sanctification without which no one will see the Lord. See to it that no one comes short of the grace of God; that no root of bitterness springing up causes trouble, and by it many be defiled; that there be no immoral or godless person like

Esau, who sold his own birthright for a single meal. For you know that even afterwards, when he desired to inherit the blessing, he was rejected, for he found no place for repentance, though he sought for it with tears.

The expression in the passage "that no root of bitterness springing up causes trouble, and by it many be defiled" (verse 15) has been taken out of context and applied to almost every bad attitude displayed by a member of the body of Christ. I've even heard a prominent seminar teacher use this text to "straighten out" people with negative attitudes. I completely agree that bad attitudes are wrong. There's no question that bitter spirits require repentance. But a close look at this verse and its context will reveal that the writer of Hebrews had something very different in mind. He was addressing a specific cause for a bitter, infectious attitude that can reap destruction.

Notice that I said "cause." The emphasis in this passage is not the *person* with the bitter spirit but the *climate* that encourages bitterness to spring up. This is borne out by the verses that immediately precede the above passage, which clearly set the tone for restoration: "Therefore, strengthen the hands that are weak and the knees that are feeble, and make straight paths for your feet, so that the limb which is lame may not be put out of joint, but rather be healed" (Hebrews 12:12–13).

If you had fallen into sin, wouldn't you like to be restored in a fellowship that had the above as a goal? I would. And I think the writer of Hebrews had that in mind too. That's why Hebrews 12:14–17 lays out three non-negotiable essentials to relating to each other as members of God's community in a broken, fragmented world. When we fail to permeate the Christian community with these three powerful and spiritual objectives, we end up rejecting our brothers and sisters. They become bitter because we have withheld God's tender compassion and mercy from them.

In a word, the point of this passage is rejection. And rejection is the result when we withhold what others deserve from us—and, indeed, what we have been required by God to give them. What we are required to give is summarized in these three words: peace, sanctification, and grace.

Pursue Peace

First we are to pursue peace, and to pursue it aggressively. In this context, it is the idea of creating an environment where conflict is resolved and relationships are mended ("with all men"). This is to be done intentionally and urgently. A peaceful, tender attitude toward our brothers and sisters in the body of Christ creates a climate for repentance and restoration. People realize that you are not going after them but that you want the wholesome, righteous peace that comes from a tender, repentant heart. You also show that you want to provide them a place to experience that peace.

Pursue Sanctification

Second, we want to pursue sanctification. The word *sanctification* carries with it the ideas of "holiness" and "purity." So how do we pursue sanctification? We are to create an environment that encourages people to experience the holiness of God. The writer was so adamant about sanctification that he added, "Without [sanctification] no one will see the Lord." That means, of course, that sin cannot and must not be tolerated in the community of the saints.

I am convinced that more of us do not experience genuine repentance because we tolerate sin and turn our eyes from it. As I said earlier, we have lost the awe and respect of God's holiness. That means we tend to accommodate sin both within our own lives and within the lives of others.

Paul says in Philippians 2:12–13, "So then, my beloved, just as you have always obeyed, not as in my presence only, but now much more in my absence, work out your salvation with fear and trembling; for it is God who is at work in you, both to will and to work for His good pleasure."

The intention of this passage is to instruct Christians that we must never lose sight of God's work in our midst. This realization should cause us to passionately demonstrate before a watching world that we have an authentic relationship with the God of the universe—and that God's signature is holiness. This is not just the personal responsibility of an individual Christian, but also the corporate responsibility of God's community, the church.

I know a man who has compromised his integrity. He has been sexually involved with a woman who is not his wife. He is well-known in the community as a Christian. I asked a friend of mine who knows this man quite well, "Have you tried to reach this brother by pointing out his sin and helping him to repent?"

My friend's response surprised me. He said that this man's sin was "between him and the Lord." This attitude is all too prevalent among Christians. As a consequence, we're walking away from our responsibility to help each other to live a holy life.

As we pursue sanctification, the responsibilities of the church and the individual dovetail with each other. Despite all the claims to the contrary in the name of "individual faith," my walk with Christ is *not* my own personal business. God has placed me in His body. The community of believers holds me accountable to live a holy life. Believers help me to conquer sin in my life. They encourage me to give an untarnished picture of my Savior before the world.

In a word, they help me to make it home before dark. So, as the church, we want to create an environment that celebrates holiness and helps people to overcome sin.

Pursue Grace

Third, we are to make sure that everyone who comes into contact with us is showered with God's grace. I love the way the writer of Hebrews put it. Look at these words in chapter 12, verse 15: "See to it that no one comes short of the grace of God."

There are two clear implications here. First, we should not withhold God's grace from anyone. Second, according to this verse, it is our obligation to make sure that others are experiencing His wonderful grace.

This indeed is an expression of the sweetness of Christ. It is the attitude that looks for the opportunity to lead others to experience the unconditional love, mercy, and forgiveness that is at the core of this thing called Christianity. The message is that when we sin, there is forgiveness. The church is more like Christ when we pour out grace on repentant members of the body. It should be our aim to welcome those who have failed, to wrap our arms around them, and to love them back to wholeness.

THE BOTTOM LINE:
WE'RE ALL FORGIVEN SERVANTS

Oh, how it breaks the heart of God to see that we push people away because we do not want to be associated with their sinfulness! We use all kinds of "biblical" smoke and mirrors to justify the rejection. The real issue is that we are embarrassed of our own sin and don't like reminders of it. We are so full of spiritual pride that we have forgotten how graciously and tenderly God deals with us when we fail.

Legalism has a severe stranglehold on the church. In Matthew 18, Jesus told the story of a king who wanted to settle accounts with his slaves. One slave owed the king an enormous sum of money—an amount so vast that there is no conceivable way he could pay the debt. On the brink of losing everything, the slave fell on his face and pleaded for forgiveness. An amazing thing happened: He experienced grace. Look at these words: "And the lord of that slave felt compassion and released him and forgave him the debt" (Matthew 18:27).

You would think that this forgiven slave would be the world's greatest ambassador for forgiveness and compassion, right? But what did he do? Jesus went on to say that the forgiven slave found another guy who owed him a fairly insignificant sum of money. He grabbed the guy and, choking him, demanded his money. The poor fellow pleaded with the forgiven slave to give him more time to get the resources together. No deal. Mister Recipient of Grace had his buddy thrown into jail.

Most of us are angered, even repulsed, by this story. We say, "How can anybody be so cold and heartless? How can anybody so quickly and easily forget God's mercy?" But we do it all the time.

A friend of mine took a lot of heat for being seen publicly with a fallen Christian leader. Some thought he was condoning his friend's actions. When I talked to him about it, he said that he stood with him because the brother had repented, and he needed someone to let him know that he was loved. Then he added, "I remember God's grace and forgiveness in my own life. I have no choice but to offer the same to a brother."

Please don't forget that you, too, have been forgiven. To withhold this grace from someone else is to ask for major trouble. A "root of bitterness" will grow and spread its contamination throughout the body. Angry, frustrated, and rejected people feel as if they have no place to go. They share their hurt, pain, and disappointment with others. Relationships are fractured, the poison is released, and the damage is done.

And that's the point of the illustration that the writer of Hebrews gave regarding Esau and Jacob. Do you remember the story? (Genesis 27:30–40). Jacob swindled his brother

Esau out of his birthright (the blessing and inheritance that belonged to the oldest son) for a meal. When Esau realized what he had done, he was crushed and could not "make things right." Broken and in tears, "he found no place for repentance" (Hebrews 12:17). He was rejected.

The point of the illustration is that the church of Jesus Christ should never allow this to happen. We must always be the place to repent. Where we offer an atmosphere of peace, accountability, holiness, and grace, we reject rejection. We hang out the shingle that says, "We welcome the repentant."

But assuming we have done our best to create a climate for repentance, how do we go about addressing and confronting sin?

CHAPTER SEVEN

The Call
to Confront

The Christian community is required to intentionally and directly confront sin. That doesn't make it easy. One poignant example of confrontation is the story recounted by Gary Rossberg, a dear friend. A woman was having an affair. Her husband knew nothing about it for some time. One day he found a letter from his wife's paramour. As he read the letter, the painful, gruesome truth crushed his heart. He felt betrayed. He was bewildered and frustrated. He wondered what went wrong. He and his wife were both Christians. They seemed to have a good marriage, and he just didn't know what had taken place. How could something like this happen to his family, to their relationship?

Before he confronted his wife, he determined he would do whatever it took not only to save their marriage, but also to plead with her to make things right with the Lord. With tears streaming down his cheeks, he confronted his wife. He said only two words: "I know." With that, the floodgates opened. She repented, and today their marriage has been restored. He won his wife.

I don't even want to imagine the courage it took for this man to confront his own wife about her sin. He showed the best responses in confronting his wife with the goal of restoring her, however. He didn't make excuses for her. Yet he confronted her in love and clearly with the attitude that he wanted to restore their marriage.

Let me say again that sin must never be minimized or tolerated. It is awful, it is destructive, and it cost God His Son. When the church fails to deal with sin, we tarnish God's reputation. We are not taken seriously by a watching world. There is no authenticity to our message because apparently there is nothing—other than our words and rituals—that distinguishes us from unbelievers. The church is then viewed as nothing more than another established institutional symbol of Western civilization.

What makes a church any different from a local tavern where the patrons gather around the bar and tell their burdens and life struggles over a vodka and tonic? Or the local support group meeting at the community center giving out large doses of affirmation and encouragement without making any "value judgement" as to whether a person's actions are right or wrong? Or the social club that prides itself in taking care of its own, creating the aura of exclusivity and special privilege?

I could go on, but you get the picture. The church of Jesus Christ exists for the transformation of lives, not for the affirmation of lifestyles. So when sin takes place in the church, we have a responsibility to deal with it.

THE FRAMEWORK FOR CONFRONTATION

Once again, the question is, How do we address and confront sin?

The head of the church Himself tells us what to do. Look at the framework that Jesus outlined in Matthew 18:15–17:

If your brother sins, go and show him his fault in private; if he listens to you, you have won your brother. But if he does not listen to you, take one or two more with you, so that by the mouth of two or three witnesses every fact may be confirmed. If he refuses to listen to them, tell it to the church; and if he refuses to listen even to the church, let him be to you as a Gentile and a tax collector.

Here, Jesus offered a four-step process for confronting sin. First, go in private to confront the person in sin. Second, take two or three witnesses with you. Third, bring the person and the sin before the church. Fourth, if there is no repentance, then the person is to be treated as if he is an unbeliever and expelled from the church.

Before we look more closely at this process, we need to remember that the goal of all of this is to "win" or restore the person back into full fellowship with God and others. That goal should shape our approach and attitude toward fallen members of the Christian community. We shouldn't be out to "get" them, but rather to win them. Jude addressed this approach when he said, "Save others, snatching them out of the fire; and on some have mercy with fear, hating even the garment polluted by the flesh" (Jude 23).

I referred earlier to the revival that took place at a recent Campus Crusade for Christ staff conference. That revival was marked by a spirit of repentance that spread throughout the entire audience. Fellow staff members, in brokenness, approached the microphone and publicly confessed their sin. They acknowledged their sin before God and sought forgiveness from their sisters and brothers in Christ.

However, several of us knew that one brother had been overcome by a particular sin. We felt that it was crucial to his healing and restoration to publicly "come clean" about what some knew and many more suspected. A few of us approached him and simply said, "If you want to go to the microphone, we will go with you." That's all it took. He, too, broke. He told his brothers and sisters the sin and pain and shame that he had caused.

My point is that this brother responded because he knew that we loved him. We did not want to "beat up on him" and dangle him in front of his colleagues as somebody not to be associated with. We wanted him to know that this was a place to repent and that we wanted him to come home. Praise God he did.

Again, this is the point of Matthew 18:15–17. Jesus gave this four-step process to win a Christian who sins. Repentance is the issue, and the process moves from the gentle to the severe. It's as if Jesus was saying that if gentler methods will do the work, methods that are more severe must not be used. Those who can be reasoned out of their sin must not be shamed out of it.

If repentance takes place, the issue is settled. You can end the process there. (Some circumstances, however, may dictate that restitution be made—or other steps be taken— to demonstrate that true repentance has taken place.)

At this point, we should also emphasize that Jesus started out by saying, "And if your brother sins." We have to remember that Jesus is speaking specifically of *sin*. Someone who does something that you do not care for is not necessarily sinning. Someone in sin is not necessarily someone who differs philosophically with you, or who does not embrace a particular conviction that you have. Let's keep in mind that Jesus is talking about *sin*, the clear disobedience to the Word of God.

I have heard horror stories of people being confronted over subjective matters. These issues have nothing to do with personal sin, but some upset person has made the violation of preferences a sin issue.

Before we confront someone, we must make sure that we have a clear biblical basis for doing so. Answer the question,

"According to the Word of God, what sin has this person committed?" Having established that sin has been committed, Jesus said that one person is to approach the offending Christian. "Go and show him his fault in private." The word *private* means just "between you and him alone."

WHAT CONFRONTATION LOOKS LIKE

Here's the picture. Someone in your circle has committed sin. You hear about it, and you discover that it is true.

At this point, you do not discuss it with anyone else. You do not even gather a group together and discuss the person's "fall" as a "prayer concern." Your motivation is not to embarrass or to in any way erect barriers to repentance. You come as an ally, not as an enemy. You fully realize that the broader the circle of people who know about the sin, the more difficult it will be for healing and restoration. So at this point, you keep it between yourself and the one who has committed sin. Your heart's desire is for him to hear and receive what you have to say. In fact, Jesus went on to say, "If he listens to you, you have won your brother." The idea of "listen" here is to allow the one being confronted to acknowledge that what you have said is true and to express sincere repentance. If there is sincere repentance, including the willingness to make things right with others who were affected by the sin, the mission has been accomplished and God has saved your brother. Rejoice!

I personally believe that there are many people out there who want to repent, who want to come home. They're waiting for somebody to come to them in love, to help them get the burden off their shoulders and to come clean. Maybe God will use you to do that. But suppose the person doesn't listen to you. Perhaps he refuses to repent or he denies the charges. In that case, Jesus said you take the next step.

Remember Matthew 18:16: "But if he does not listen to you, take one or two more with you, so that by the mouth of two or three witnesses every fact may be confirmed."

Here Jesus was quoting from Deuteronomy 19:15 concerning God's requirements for charges made about sin: "A single witness shall not rise up against a man on account of any iniquity or sin which he has committed; on the evidence of two or three witnesses a matter shall be confirmed."

One purpose for bringing a few witnesses is to lend further objectivity to the issue. Let's face it: Sometimes when we fall into sin, we simply do not get it. It may be because we are in denial or we need the kind of wake-up call that multiple witnesses can give. In other instances, there is willful rebellion and the refusal to own up to the sin. A gentle but clear and firm confirmation is in order. In still other cases, one witness may be wrong, and the requirement of additional witnesses can keep the false witness from ruining someone's reputation.

The presence and acknowledgement of two or three witnesses gives the message that you are not the only one who is aware of the sin. But we must not forget the purpose of the visit. We do not want to prove our point or to win an argument. The goal is to win our brother. Remember, we want him back home. The attitude and approach is crucial. We want him to experience genuine repentance. Again, this group of you and one or two others come as allies and not enemies. If the brother in sin repents at this stage, the mission is accomplished and you rejoice.

The Process

A few years ago, I noticed that a married friend of mine was a little too familiar with other women. You know what I mean: hugs that lasted a little too long, conversations that were a little too personal, inappropriate comments, and too much time alone with women other than his wife. Although at the time I did not have any objective proof that he was doing anything sinful, I certainly felt that his behavior was foolish and dangerous. He was asking for trouble, and I told him so.

I must admit I was surprised at his defensiveness. In essence, he told me that I should mind my own business. He said that I had become a victim of legalism. I left our brief meeting stung by his response, but even more troubled that something was definitely wrong.

I began to pray fervently for him, asking God to show him that he was walking on thin ice and that he needed to step back onto safe ground before he fell through. I prayed that, if in fact he had already fallen, God would make it known to those of us who love him and are committed to him.

Several weeks went by. Then the dreaded evidence came to my attention. It was confirmed that he had committed sin with several of these women. Once again I met with him in private, but this time with the evidence. I told him that I was his friend, and I wanted to stand with him through this if he was willing to repent. He dug in his heels. Emotionally he pushed me away—and then he exploded. In not-so-subtle terms, he told me that I couldn't prove anything and that what he did with his life was between himself and God. He asked me to leave. I felt hurt and rejected. As I walked away, I was heartbroken that my friend was so apparently willing to destroy his marriage, damage his family, and forsake his friends in the ministry for the momentary pleasures of sin. But I was also very angry at the devil and the self-deception that is a trademark of unrepentant sin.

Still more time passed. By this time, a few others knew about the charges and the evidence, so I asked to meet with him again. To my surprise, he agreed. This time I took two of these witnesses with me. Once again he was confronted with the charges and the evidence. Although he was not as volatile as before, the result was pretty much the same. He quietly listened and even admitted that he had sinned. But then he retreated to a defensive posture. Again, he made it clear that what he did was his business. In essence, he said that at this point he wasn't going to change. We pleaded with him to face his sin and to deal with it. His response was bone chilling. There wasn't a hint of remorse, much less anything that even resembled repentance.

The Final Step

Well, what do you do when the person will not respond to you and the one or two other witnesses accompanying you? Matthew 18:17 says that the next step is to tell it to the church. Notice the progression. First it's one to one. Then it's a few to one. Finally it is many to one. God's heart is to restore people, not to hurt or to embarrass us. Therefore, He gives us every opportunity to run from our sin and into His arms. But sin is stubborn, and the human heart is full of pride. As I said earlier, if gentler methods will not work, then more severe methods must be used, and God prescribes the method: "Tell it to the church."

The point is that with broader exposure perhaps the offender will wake up, face the reality of what he has done, turn from it, and be fully restored. There has been some disagreement as to what "tell it to the church" refers to. Does it mean to expose the sin and the individual to the established, appointed leaders of the church such as the deacons and elders? Some people reason that since these leaders serve as representatives of the local congregation, it carries with it the same import as exposing the matter to the entire church. However, I don't believe that this conclusion is consistent with the spirit of the passage. Jesus did not say to discuss it with the established leadership of the church; He said to tell it to the church. The reason the church needs to know is that other attempts to lovingly bring the person to a point of repentance have failed. Therefore, the sin needs to be made known throughout the congregation.

Obviously, the church leaders are accountable and responsible before God to make sure that the matter is handled in a godly, biblical, and sensitive way. A person who knows of sin in the congregation, and who has followed the previous steps with the person who is in sin, should tell the church leadership so that they can bring the matter to the church. But Jesus says that the church must know. Once again the goal is not for the offender to feel as if he is being ganged up on but to communicate God's love and mercy and that the church is a safe place, a place to repent.

Practicing loving biblical discipline takes courage. One of the reasons I believe God is withholding His hand from sending the kind of all-encompassing national revival that so many of us are praying for is that we, the church, refuse to deal biblically with sin. The awe and fear of God are absent. Holiness has become a detached, purely academic discussion presented with little, if any, appeal to obedience. In too many cases, greater holiness is preached as if it is totally unattainable in this life.

Church discipline is supposed to be a visible reminder to all members that any of us are susceptible to sin. It should cause believers to fear the power and the shame of sin and the consequent public exposure of unrepented sin. When we do not practice the kind of church discipline that Jesus outlines, people tend to lose their appreciation for the awful devastation of sin. Most tragically, they lose their appreciation of the power of Calvary to cleanse and conquer sin even in this life.

No More Options

My late pastor, Dr. Herman Conely, believed in applying Matthew 18:15–17. Evidently he had followed the procedure outlined in the text with one of the members of the church. Because there was a refusal to repent, he had no other choice than to tell the matter to the church. He challenged the congregation to pray for repentance and restoration to take place. The next Sunday the individual involved came to church, and at the end of the service he publicly confessed his sin and repented. Pastor Conely then loving-

ly but directly reminded us that the sin had been taken care
of and that but for the grace of God, we are all capable of
doing what this person did—if not worse. I don't think
that there was a dry eye in the church that Sunday. It is an
incredibly moving experience to see someone come home.

What happens if the person refuses to listen to the
church? Suppose he pushes away the attempts of the fellowship of believers to win him back? Well, Jesus said there's
only one thing left to do. Our Lord's prescribed options have
been rejected. There's no repentance. Jesus said in the second half of verse 17, "And if he refuses to listen even to the
church, let him be to you as a Gentile and a tax collector."

Notice the emphatic statement "even to the church." It
is as if Jesus was saying, "If you're going to listen to anybody, you ought to listen to those who love you, care about
you, and share a common faith." So far, the person has rejected the individual, the other witnesses, and the
church—the very place that exists to love and nurture him
to wholeness. This person is therefore to be treated "as a
Gentile and tax collector." Remember, Jesus was speaking
from a Jewish context. In other words, just as Gentiles
(non-Jews) do not share in the unique relationship that
Jews have because the Jews are God's chosen people, so
also every Christian who refuses to repent is acting as if he
does not have a relationship with God. Not only that, sin is
repulsive to God and ought to be repulsive to His people.
So willful, unrepenting Christians ought to be treated like
the unscrupulous tax collectors. These tax gatherers were
notorious, legalized thieves. In the name of collecting rev-
enue for the Roman Empire, they skimmed off the top,
lined their own pockets, and generally had lavish lifestyles.

Problem: Their evil ways caused them to be rejected
and confined to a lonely and isolated life. Do you get the
picture? *When we refuse and reject God's attempts to win our
hearts by calling us to repentance, we are acting as if we are not
related to Him.* Because grace has been rejected, the unre-

pentant person is to be removed from the fellowship of the church.

Matthew Henry described the prescribed treatment of an unrepentant sinner this way: "Cast out of the communion of the church, secluded from special ordinances, degraded from the dignity of a church member that he may be ashamed of his sin and they [the other Christians] may not be infected by it."

Let me quickly say that removing the unrepentant from the fellowship of the church is the last resort. If it must be done, it ought to be done with a sense of sadness and loss. Any leader or group of people who can remove a person from the fellowship of a church with a sense of gladness is, in my opinion, perverted and as guilty as that unrepentant person, if not worse.

You're probably wondering what happened to my friend who was taken through steps one and two of this process. To me it's a very sad story. As of this writing and to my knowledge, he has yet to repent. The issue was taken to the leadership of the Christian organization he represented. They handled it in a very responsible way. Once again he refused to face his sin and repent. He was terminated.

What's even more disappointing is that although he was a member of a church, his church refused to deal with his sin. It relegated its responsibility to the Christian organization. I've often wondered, if the organization and the church had worked together, both exercising their God-given responsibility, if we would not have been able to reclaim a brother.

But there still is another very important issue. If we're going to give people a place to repent, we must not only create the environment for repentance to take place (Hebrews 12:14–17), and follow the pattern given to us by Jesus Himself (Matthew 18:15–17), but we must also be very careful how we approach those who have sinned.

CHAPTER EIGHT

Attitude Counts

The Christian community is required to have a right attitude in restoring repentant brothers and sisters. A pastor friend of mine told me the story of one of his staff members who was caught visiting pornographic sites on the Internet. When he was confronted, it was as if a burden had been taken off his shoulders. He confessed that he had struggled with an addiction to pornography for years.

Ultimately this is a wonderful story. No, not because he sinned; that's terrible. But he has repented and is being restored. He has embraced the shame and embarrassment that his sin has caused. He is responding because of the love and grace he feels from the leaders in the church. He knows that they are committed to him and to his family.

And what does that commitment look like? The church is not sweeping his sin under the carpet. By no means is that fellowship ignoring or minimizing the horrible nature of what he has done. He's willing to do whatever's necessary to make things right and to overcome his sinful addiction. And to the credit of the leadership of the church, they are applying biblical discipline in the spirit of grace with a view toward wholeness and spiritual healing. May their tribe increase!

It's that type of redemptive attitude and approach to restoring those of us who fail that I want to talk about in this chapter.

ATTITUDE CHECK

The apostle Paul gave us a sobering warning in Galatians 6:1: "Brethren, even if anyone is caught in any trespass, you who are spiritual, restore such a one in a spirit of gentleness; each one looking to yourself, so that you too will not be tempted."

We all know that *how* you do something is sometimes as important as *what* you do. For example, I am privileged to be the father of four children. I have learned the hard way that I can't always say the same thing the same way to each of my children and get the same result. They are different. Each one has an individual personality, so each one responds differently. If I want to get my message through, then I have to keep in mind the "address" of that particular child. This is especially true when I have to confront them or correct them. I must communicate in such a way that the message is clearly heard. They must know that *they* are not the problem but that *what they have done* is the issue. Therefore, they must also know that the behavior (sin) must be corrected.

This is Paul's point in Galatians 6:1. He separated the sin from the individual. Look closely at the approach, the attitude. The apostle said that if someone is caught in "any trespass," our attitude ought to be the same. The sin does not determine the attitude. Whether it is adultery, stealing, dishonesty, or murder makes no difference. We must address the one guilty of ("caught in") the sin with an attitude rooted in integrity and authenticity. Paul said that there are four perspectives that comprise this attitude.

NURTURING THE ATTITUDE THAT RESTORES

First, before we approach anybody about sin, we must make sure that we have a consistent, growing relationship with the Lord. The only person qualified to confront another about sin is the one who is overcoming sin in his own life. That's why Paul identified that person or group of people as "you who are spiritual." Again, Paul was not talking about perfection but about a progressive walk with Christ in which there is growth and holiness, the absence of hypocrisy.

A man once told me that he was confronted by a friend of his concerning a sin he had committed. He said that he had a very difficult time swallowing what his friend was saying. It wasn't because his friend wasn't telling him the truth, but because he knew that his friend was a hypocrite. He said to me, "Crawford, I knew I was wrong, but this guy wasn't clean either. He needed a bath as much as I did!" Let's make sure that we are washed before we tell somebody else to clean up.

Second, we must keep in mind the objective: "*Restore* such a one" (italics added). The word *restore* comes from a Greek medical term that was used in reference to setting a broken bone. What a graphic and appropriate picture of what we are called to do!

Confrontation is always painful. Paul was saying that we must tell the direct, painful truth to someone who has sinned. No doubt about it, it will hurt. I have never suffered a broken bone, but I have had stitches on several occasions. Each time the doctor warned me it was going to hurt. However, the doctor's primary objective was *not* to hurt me, but to repair me. In order to fix me, there had to be some pain.

Sin always involves pain. It caused God pain when it was committed. It caused our Savior pain when He cured it. And it causes us pain when it is corrected. Please keep in mind when you have the responsibility of approaching someone concerning sin, that you are not there to give the person a piece of your mind, straighten out an embarrassing situation, or do damage control. Instead, you are on a mission of restoration. Identify the destination (a restored relationship with God and His people), and clearly, specifically tell the person the painful truth.

Third, our approach is to be wrapped in gentleness ("in a spirit of gentleness"). Let's go back to the example of a doctor. Just as a doctor who has to tell a patient some bad news will take into account the emotional and psychological state of the patient, so we too must carefully and gently "break the news" to the person who has sinned that we are aware of the sin.

The prophet Nathan is a wonderful illustration of gently approaching a fallen brother. You know the story. David, the greatest king Israel ever had, had known the blessing and favor of God in ways that most of us will never experience. He was called "a man after [God's] own heart," but he sinned. David committed adultery and murder. Just when he thought that his sin was tightly and securely covered, Nathan showed up.

Nathan didn't approach King David spouting fire and brimstone. No, he gently painted David a heartrending, compelling word picture of a wealthy herdsman who took advantage of a very poor man. The king was incensed that anyone would be that cruel. Then Nathan uttered those famous words, "You are the man!" (2 Samuel 12:7).

You see, Nathan understood that his mission was not to denounce David, but to be used of God to help David own up to what he had done. Gentleness was in order. But notice, gentleness does not mean a lack of courage or shrinking back from telling the complete truth. Nathan was clear in his communication, and King David got the message. Broken by the shame and guilt of his sin, David said six words that ushered in repentance and relief: "I have sinned against the Lord" (verse 13). The point is simply this: If and when it becomes your responsibility to confront someone because of sin, take some time to prayerfully think through how you too can clearly but gently break the news.

Fourth, before we approach someone concerning sin, we are to keep in mind that we have the *potential* to do the same thing. In other words, we are to approach those "caught in any trespass" not as if we have a right to do so, but filled with the realization that we also have been forgiven. We come pointing to the sufficiency, forgiveness, and grace that is found in Christ. Contrast that with a finger-pointing, condescending attitude that says, "You need to get your act together like I have or you're history."

AN ATTITUDE OF CAUTION

When we think about approaching someone about their sin, however, it is absolutely crucial that we do everything we can to get our facts straight.

Not too long ago, a Sunday school superintendent I know was driving through a section of her community that was lined with bars and adult bookstores. To her shock, she thought she saw the chairman of the deacon board on his way into one of the bars. She nearly ran into the back of the car ahead of her when she did a double take to make sure of his identity. There was no mistaking who it was.

She kept the matter to herself for a few days. She wondered whether she should confront the deacon herself. She wondered what good it would do if she did. She knew the command of the Lord in Scripture to do just that, but she wondered, *Had she really caught the deacon in sin?*

All sorts of thoughts went through her mind. Was the deacon an undiscovered alcoholic? Was he carrying on an illicit affair and making that bar his point of rendezvous? Did he frequent that section of town, and perhaps take in the adult bookstores while he was there?

Please take note. Even at this point, had she gone to the

deacon in question, she might have settled her mind one way or the other fairly quickly. Still, that Sunday she was ready to go to the pastor with her concern.

When the service came to a point of prayer, a young man stood up in the row behind her. It was the deacon's son, there with his mother and father. She hadn't seen him in church for years. He'd gone off to the military, and then seemed to drop off the face of the earth. The young man began slowly. "It's been a long time since I've been with you here for a Sunday morning. Too long. But I'd like to give a testimony of thankfulness today for my parents. Especially my dad. He came to talk to me while I was in a bar the other day, half-drunk. He took me home and cleaned me up. I'd like to publicly thank God for him and Mom, and ask for your prayers as I go into a rehab center to begin treatment tomorrow."

The Sunday school superintendent breathed a sigh of relief, and she prayed fervently in the next few moments for the deacon and his family. Then she prayed that God would help her remember to take Him at His Word about such situations in the future.

RECOVERING CORRECT ATTITUDES

Whenever we hear of sin in the Christian community, it ought to produce in us a sense of sadness, humility, and self-examination. None of us are immune. We overcome by God's amazing grace.

Many years ago, a friend asked me to pray for him because he had to confront someone about a sin in his life. He told me that he could not believe that someone could do something so foolish and stupid. As I listened to him, I detected no small amount of pride. I asked him if he had the ability to do what his friend did. Further, I asked if he had ever done anything that someone else would put into the category of foolish and stupid. He lowered his head in embarrassment and said, "Thanks, Crawford. I get the message."

If it becomes my turn to be confronted because of sin in my life, I would much rather have someone come alongside me in love and point to the one who died for *all* of our sins and who reclaims and cleanses *all* of us who turn from our sin to Him.

We have lost too many wounded and wandering warriors because in many instances, oddly enough, the church has not been a place to repent. We have not often addressed sin biblically, nor have we carried a proper attitude toward those caught in sin.

No, we are not responsible for another person's sinful choices and actions. But we are responsible before God to obey and apply the clear teaching of the Word of God in responding to those who fail. Can they come home? Is there a place for the repentant in your communion? Do you know of anyone who has withdrawn from you and other Christians because he or she is living in sin and suspects you know about it? Lovingly pursue that person and ask God to use you to help him or her to make it home before dark.

CHAPTER NINE

Pilgrim's Predicament

I have a confession to make. If I have to drive somewhere and it takes more than three hours to get there, then I get antsy. My wife says I am worse with the issue of travel impatience than our children were when they were young.

You know the situation. Karen and I lovingly armed our children with coloring books, crayons, reading books, and handy snack foods as we piled in the car for a family trip. Our children were fully and quietly occupied for, say, three minutes from the time we left our driveway. Then the questions began.

"Dad, are we there yet?"

"No, Honey. Over there is the McDonalds we go to on Saturdays. I know they all look alike, but our drive today is just starting. Say, does that coloring book have a picture of a chipmunk in it? I'd love a picture of a chipmunk that you'd colored especially for my office."

"When are we going to get there?"

"A little while after you've finished that picture, Sweetheart."

We learned quickly that we had to keep giving them progress reports, encouraging them that we were getting closer to our destination. For some reason, we found the progress reports to be important for our sense of well-being, too. These reports, along with a few other things to occupy their minds, gave them a sense of hope. Each passing minute (assuming we were not stuck in traffic) and every mile we traveled (assuming we were not lost) meant that we were going somewhere. Barring any unforeseen incident, we would get to our destination.

Yes, that perspective helps even me, the impatient traveler. Focusing on where we're going not only puts into perspective where we are, but it also tends to help us give our attention to what is really important along the journey. This was the apostle John's point when he said, "Beloved, now we are children of God, and it has not appeared as yet what we will be. We know that when He appears, we will be like Him, because we will see Him just as He is. And everyone who has his hope fixed on Him purifies himself, just as He is pure" (1 John 3:2–3).

John identified the destination as "we will be like Him." No, we are not completely like Jesus yet—but that's where we're going. We're moving toward Him. One day we will shed the sin and imperfections of this life, and we will be completely without sin. We will fully realize and experience the full righteousness of Christ.

We have all been encouraged and impressed by great godly men and women who model Christ's likeness before us. We should both admire and seek to follow them as they follow Christ. They are God's gifts to us. They motivate us to keep looking to the sufficiency of the Savior for all that we need in this life.

Personally, my "hall of faith" includes my pastor during my teen years, Burton Cathie, who not only led me to the Savior but also modeled before me a life of faith and godly consistency; Mrs. Margaret Ponder, whose prayer life brings conviction to my soul and also has encouraged me to cry out to God in believing prayer for all of my needs and the concerns of my heart; Bill Bright, whose humility and godliness is a refreshing reminder that to be an effective Christian leader and to embrace brokenness are not a contradiction in terms; Robertson McQuilkin, whose example of Christlike love and leadership in his home and in the Christian community has taught me that true greatness means to give it all up and to place oneself completely at God's disposal.

Many others in my life—and in yours—are further along the journey than we are. These saints' lives shout that incredible progress toward the holiness of God can be made. Others have passed from this life into the arms of a waiting Savior. For them the journey is complete. They are home, and they have left sin, temptation, and the pull of the kingdom of darkness behind. They fully realize and experience the righteousness of Christ. But we are still here. We are still on the journey. Sin reminds us that we are not there yet. But the certainty of our arriving at our destination ought to motivate us to be serious and to get busy with working on overcoming sin now.

SIN: THE HERE-AND-NOW ISSUE

We are called to overcome sin with a sense of urgency. In fact, our full-time occupation as Christians is to press toward Christlikeness in every area of our lives:

> That I may know Him and the power of His resurrection and the fellowship of His sufferings, being conformed to His death; in order that I may attain to the resurrection from the dead. Not that I have already obtained it or have already become perfect, but I press on that I may lay hold of that for which I was laid hold of by Christ Jesus. Brethren, I do not regard myself as having laid hold of it yet; but one thing I do: forgetting what lies behind and reaching forward to what lies ahead, I press on to-

ward the goal for the prize of the upward call of God in Christ Jesus. *(Philippians 3:10–14)*

"Pressing on" is a two-way process: As we work on our lives, He works through our lives. It is a lifelong assignment. But the problem is that we sometimes get lazy along the way. A little compromise here, a little compromise there, and before you know it we find ourselves at a place we did not intend to be. So how do we make progress on the journey? How do we stay on task?

I believe the answer is found in properly responding to the Light. The apostle John, based on his up-close-and-personal experience with the Savior, summarized the testimony and life message of Jesus in one clear, riveting statement: "This is the message we have heard from Him and announce to you, that God is Light, and in Him there is no darkness at all" (1 John 1:5).

Consider that last phrase "no darkness at all" for a moment. This is a statement of God's brilliance, His utter perfection; in a word, His holiness. John's point is that the life and ministry of Jesus pointed to, demonstrated, and exemplified the light of God. Further, just as when Jesus walked the face of this earth He called people to respond to the Light, so He calls all of us today to respond to His brilliance, His holiness.

In the previous chapters, we laid out a challenge for the church to be a place that hangs out a shingle to welcome repentant sinners. This is a vital part of restoring people to biblical wholeness. In fact, we must understand the church as a fellowship of repentant sinners, from the most visible leader to the quietest newcomer.

The issue of fellowship certainly was not lost on the early church. In fact, the theme of 1 John is fellowship. The culture around the early church understood "fellowship" as "sharing or experiencing that which we have in common" or as "living in partnership."

Throughout his first letter to the early church, John told us how to live in fellowship with God and with each other. As we saw in the verse above, John clearly—and very early in the letter—gave us the standard of our fellowship: God's perfect holiness.

PILGRIM'S PREDICAMENT:
RESPONDING TO THE LIGHT

After making clear the standard, John then proceeded to give us four responses we can make to the Light. Three of the responses are negative. They will tend to fragment our very being instead of leading us to wholeness in Jesus Christ. As we will see, each of these negative responses is preceded by the conditional expression "If we say . . ."

False Practice

The first of these negative responses is *false practice*. Pay close attention to 1 John 1:6: "If we say that we have fellowship with Him and yet walk in the darkness, we lie and do not practice the truth." John was bringing some pretty strong stuff to the table here! He said that if we declare to others that we have a relationship with God and yet our lives are consistently characterized by sin, then we are lying. Why? Because we are not living out what we say we possess.

John was not talking about an inability to achieve sinless perfection. Instead, he was addressing the issue of habitual, unrepentant sin. One key in this verse is the expression "walk in the darkness." The verb "walk" is in the present tense. This suggests continuous activity associated with the darkness—if you will, an ongoing relationship with sin. "Walking in darkness" means we're comfortable with the darkness. We live as if we belong to the darkness. If this is so, then there is room to question whether or not we have a relationship with God.

Church membership and saying all the right words are no evidence of a genuine relationship with the Savior. I believe that our churches are full of people who sing the songs, say the prayers, and read the Scriptures—*but who have no relationship with the Light.* They know the spiritual routine, but their lives are characterized by darkness. They have no genuine remorse in their hearts when they sin. They seem to be comfortable with broken relationships and bitter, unforgiving attitudes. Their lifestyles and habits on their jobs, in their homes, and even in church fellowship are more of a testimony to the darkness than to the Light Himself.

Think of it this way: Suppose you spent some time with my wife Karen and me, then began to observe our four children. I believe you would soon notice a Loritts "mark" somewhere on or about our children. Perhaps you would see that one bore a physical resemblance to me, whereas another looked like Karen. Maybe you'd pick up on a habit or attitude that would cause you to think, *That sure reminds me of Karen,* or *That's something that Crawford would do.* You know something? That's the way it should be, because our children are related to us.

In the same way, if we have genuinely experienced a new birth, then the light of God's holiness—that which is the essence of our heavenly Father—will mark our lives. It really makes it impossible for us to habitually live in unrepentant darkness and say that we have a partnership with the Light.

A False Perspective

The second response is a *false perspective.* In this situation, we don't see what God sees, and we ignore what His Light reveals about us. First John 1:8 says, "If we say that we have no sin, we are deceiving ourselves and the truth is not in us."

Here John was speaking of our capacity to cross the line and sin. He was not talking about specific *acts of* sin, but the *ability to* sin. John's point is it is impossible to catch a glimpse of God's perfect holiness and then conclude that we are like God. God's Light reveals our awful ability to violate His commandments, hurt His heart, and do damage to others and ourselves. His Light exposes every imperfection about us. Nothing is hidden from Him.

This should be a clear warning: *We should never lie to ourselves about our potential to do evil.*

I sometimes think that our emphasis on self-esteem is pushed a little too far. We have to be careful that, as we celebrate the wonder and marvel of the human spirit, we do not minimize what God says about all of us. We are sinners. We come fully furnished with the ability to do the most horrendous, despicable things imaginable.

This awareness should fill our hearts with a sense of gratitude and deep appreciation for the wonderful grace of God. Oddly enough, as we discussed earlier, we are closest to God's heart when we realize how much we need grace and how far we have to go to even begin to reflect His holiness. But because sin is rooted in pride, it is very easy for us to fall victim to the self-deception that we are better than we really are. The apostle Paul was well aware of that tendency in each of us. That's why he warned the Corinthian church, "Therefore let him who thinks he stands take heed that he does not fall" (1 Corinthians 10:12).

Understand what I'm saying here. We can certainly live the Christian life with confidence and the assurance that God is able to keep us and sustain us. We serve a God who is more than sufficient. He is "able to do exceeding abundantly beyond all that we ask or think" (Ephesians 3:20).

But we are in danger when we trust in our own strength, insights, and abilities to live the Christian life. Pride takes over. We're blinded to our capacity to sin. We become our own "light," and we fall. Former televangelist and founder of the PTL ministry, Jim Bakker, and one of his top executives, Richard Dortsch, both wrote books related to the PTL scandal of the late 1980s. Their books not only chronicled the events related to the scandal, but also outlined their paths to repentance and restoration. What struck me as I read these books is that both Bakker and Dortsch said that *things began to unravel when they shifted their focus from God to "what they were doing for Him."*

Ever so subtly, they wandered from the Light into self-deception. Pride took over. It was only a matter of time before the bottom fell out. The ministry came tumbling down, families were torn apart, and both had to embrace the shame and disgrace of sin. The same thing will happen to any of us who ignore the Light and choose to deny what the Light says about us. *The "beginning of the end" is when we deny or minimize our capacity to do what is wrong.*

A False Pronouncement

The third response is a *false pronouncement.* I have two older sisters. When we were growing up and our parents went out, my sisters were left in charge. I never liked this arrangement because when Pop wasn't there, I considered myself to be "the man of the house." When I reminded my sisters of this crucial fact, they agreed that I was the man of the house. But then they would say, "You're just not in charge. We are."

One evening when our parents were out, I was swinging my baseball bat in the living room. That was the first problem, of course. My mother had told me time and again, "Never swing the bat in the house."

Swinging the bat in spite of her clear command already put me in the realm of false practice. I would have certainly claimed to have had close fellowship with my mother at the time—but my putting the bat in motion in defiance of her showed that I didn't love her as I should have at that moment. Believing our living room was Yankee Stadium was certainly a false perspective, as was my firmly held belief that it was only *other* kids who were clumsy enough to actually damage something by swinging a bat indoors.

You can imagine what happened next. I was too close to the end table on a three-and-two pitch in the bottom of the ninth with the bases loaded. As I swung that bat, fully ready to clear the left-field fence, I knocked the lamp off the table. It shattered into a hundred pieces. I quickly hid the bat.

My sisters were in another part of the house. When they heard the crash, they ran into the living room and saw the demolished lamp. They asked me what had happened.

I lied. I told them that I was minding my own business. I said somehow, mysteriously, the lamp had fallen off the table. For some reason, they said they didn't believe me. When my parents came home, I told them the same story. For some reason, they didn't believe me either.

My father knew I wasn't telling the truth. He pressed the issue. As he kept firing questions at me, I began to realize how stupid my answers sounded. I felt guilty because I *was* guilty. Finally I broke and told them the real story.

Don't deny what you know is true. In 1 John 1:10 the apostle said, "If we say that we have not sinned, we make Him a liar and His word is not in us."

Here, John said that we not only have the capacity *to do* wrong, we, in fact, *have done* wrong. When we look at God's perfect standard of holiness and the Light that emanates from His holiness, we are forced into a two-part declaration: First, we are not like He is. Second, we do things that He would not do.

We're guilty sinners. The Light of God has caught all of us with our hands in the moral cookie jar. And we are very proficient at sin. We sin by what we do, and we sin by what we fail to do. We sin with our attitudes. We sin with our thoughts. We sin with our tongues. We sin with our hands. We sin with our feet. We sin with our eyes.

You get the picture. We do what comes naturally for us, and that is to commit sin. Sin flows out of our nature. We sin because that's who we are. We are sinners.

But that isn't to say we cannot overcome sin in everyday life.

CHAPTER TEN

Pilgrim's Progress

It wasn't the apostle John's purpose to leave us in a predicament with the statement of 1 John 1:10 when he said, "If we say that we have not sinned, we make Him a liar and His word is not in us."

Reading on in his letter, you'll find out that John was *not* saying that since we are sinners, we are doomed to sin. John *certainly* wasn't saying that since we will likely sin, we shouldn't try to overcome it. (Believe it or not, I have actually heard people use this verse to excuse their sinful actions.) Rather, John was acknowledging the depths and pervasive nature of sin in our lives.

Although I do not believe that sinless perfection is possible in this life, I believe that the more we walk in fellowship with Christ, the less we should sin. As we will see shortly, God is more than able to help us overcome sin in our lives.

Mosquitoes are annoying anytime. But in some areas of the world, they carry diseases that make them mortal enemies. Most of my friends who have traveled overseas will tell you that malaria is an experience worth avoiding. My friends helped strike a proper respect of mosquitoes into me years ago during my first visit to Kenya in East Africa. It wasn't as though I hadn't taken proper precautions through medication, spray, and netting. But I still had the feeling that if I could avoid being bitten, I'd be better off.

Of course, I had an encounter with a battalion of mosquitoes my first night there. Within seconds of shutting my eyes to fall asleep, I heard the high-pitched whine of a mosquito around my ears. It landed. I swatted it. A few seconds later, another came in for a landing. It landed. I swatted it too.

But they kept coming. One would land on me and I would swat it. Then I'd have a brief reprieve until another was sent on a suicide mission. I remember thinking, *This is ridiculous. I'll be doing this all night long.* Then another thought occurred to me: *Well, each time I kill one, there will be one less mosquito in the room.*

That's the way we have to view our sin if we are going to overcome it. We have to deal with it head-on, one thought or action at a time. We must deal decisively with sin. Otherwise, it may infect us in such a way that we become incapacitated. This head-on, decisive, and constant action against sin leads to the only true and right response to the light of God.

In summary, as we look at the perfect standard of God's holiness that John pointed to in 1 John 1:5, we have four responses. Three of them are negative responses: First, we cannot say that we have a relationship with the God of light if our lives are characterized by darkness (verse 6). Second, we cannot look at the perfect standard and then say and act as if we are not capable of sin (verse 8). Third, as we compare our lives to God's requirements for holiness, we cannot conclude that we have not committed acts of sin (verse 10).

So that leaves us with the true and right response to the light of God: repentance.

REPENTANCE: THE PILGRIM'S PROGRESS

The apostle John gave us one of the best descriptive definitions of *repentance* that you will find anywhere in the Bible. John presented repentance in its two parts, both as a *point* and as a *process*. Here's where the battle is won or lost. I believe that a lot of Christians confine themselves to years of struggling with a particular sin not because they have not embraced *points* of repentance, but because they have not embarked on the *process* of repentance.

Suppose my car engine burned up because I didn't keep enough oil in it. My mechanic would say to me, "Crawford, because you didn't take care of the oil when you should have, you will now have to spend a small fortune to buy a new engine."

Preventative maintenance would have saved me from heartache, not to mention a lot of money. So it is with our walk with Christ. Repentance does not just involve the *point* at which we turn from the sin, but it also means the *process* of walking away from sin toward the light of God. This is God's preventative maintenance.

In 1 John 1:9 we see the *point* of repentance: confession. When we gaze at God's perfect standard of holiness, we must come clean. Verse 9 describes what that looks like: "If we confess our sins, He is faithful and righteous to forgive us our sins and to cleanse us from all unrighteousness."

The key word here is "confess," which literally means to "say the same thing." The obvious question here is, "Who must I agree with regarding my sins?" The obvious answer is, "God."

We have to agree with God concerning our sin. That means we say exactly the same thing that God says about what we have done. We don't excuse it. We don't use nice-sounding "weasel" words to make sin sound more acceptable. We don't retreat to the denial of false practice, false perspective, or false pronouncement. We look at the Light and the specific sin we have committed, and we say what God says: We're guilty.

These days, it seems it just isn't popular to embrace personal responsibility for our actions. Regrettably, this is true even in some parts of the Christian community. We tend to dilute personal sin and evil by blaming outside contributing factors for our flawed behavior. It could well be that our background, or events and circumstances over which we have no control, contributes to our propensity to commit certain sins. We may indeed need to identify those factors to strengthen our resolve to overcome certain temptations. But make no mistake: We sin because we sin.

Years ago, I had the sad responsibility as a leader to help set forth the framework to confront and restore a brother who had been caught in adultery. Someone suggested that the first thing we needed to do was to get this person to a professional counselor as quickly as possible. Then he might understand why he did what he did.

I responded by saying, "No, I think the first thing we need to do is to lovingly approach him and see if he owns up to what he has done. The first order of business is for him to experience the cleansing and forgiveness of God that comes as a result of the sincere confession of sin."

We cannot experience the cleansing and forgiveness of God if we don't completely take responsibility for what we have done. I cannot stress this strongly enough. When we come to God concerning sin we have committed, we cannot say, "I have sinned, *but* . . ." Biblical confession of sin demands that I present the sin, and my responsibility for committing the sin, before God. Biblical confession of sin is done without qualifications, excuses, or additional information that would at least in my mind insulate me from facing the reality and personal ownership for my actions.

True confession takes utter and complete sincerity. We confess our sins not because we have been caught in doing something that is wrong, but because we are sincerely sorry for what we have done. That's the bottom line of these words from the apostle Paul to the early church in Corinth: "For the sorrow that is according to the will of God produces a repentance without regret, leading to salvation, but the sorrow of the world produces death" (2 Corinthians 7:10).

Hear this again: Godly sorrow is more than feeling bad that you've been caught in sin. Godly sorrow actually produces a desire in you to change, because you know what you've done is wrong. When you want to experience cleansing and forgiveness, repentance is the route to take—and that includes sorrow for your sin.

There's a profound difference between sorrow over sin and sorrow over being caught. It's like the little boy who went into a toy store intending to steal a state-of-the-art water gun. He made his way to the water gun aisle. He looked cautiously around him. There was no one in sight. This was too easy! He took the gun, hid it inside his jacket, and casually walked toward the door.

The problem was that since the boy didn't see any people in the water gun aisle, he also never noticed the security camera there. His little heist had been caught on film. As he walked to the front entrance, the security guard stopped him. He took the boy to the security center and pointed to a monitor. There, the little boy saw the video of himself stealing the gun, and he began to cry. But the guard said, "Son, stop crying. You're not sorry that you stole the water gun. You're just sorry that you got caught."

Too many people have the idea that the confession of sin is a sort of "release valve" for the pressure we feel when we know we've sinned. We use confession as a way of getting out of God's doghouse. We have no sincere desire to overcome the sin. We want to ease our minds, but not change our behavior. But 1 John 1:9 is not a pacifier to soothe us as we continue to repeat the sin. When we come to God with a sincere, broken heart concerning the sin we have committed, He makes us clean and affirms in our souls that we are forgiven. Praise God!

Please let me encourage you to examine your heart and your motives when you come to the Lord to confess your sins. Do it from a heart full of sincerity, and He will launch you on a path of wholeness and victory.

But, remember, confession is only the first part, or again the *point,* of repentance. To sincerely confess your sin does not necessarily mean that you will overcome that sin quickly or easily.

In truth, I don't know of a Christian who has not had the experience of repeatedly confessing to God the same sin. At times in my walk with the Lord, in deep frustration, I have cried out, "How come it's taking me so long to get better? Why do I have to come back to the Lord with this same sin?"

I know that we will struggle with our weaknesses until we are in the presence of God. But those weaknesses don't set aside God's desire for us to overcome sin in this life!

WALKING: THE PILGRIM'S PROCESS

The way we overcome specific sins we commit is by embracing the *process* of repentance. Take a closer look at 1 John 1:7: "But if we walk in the Light as He Himself is in the Light, we have fellowship with one another, and the blood of Jesus His Son cleanses us from all sin."

The key expression here is "walk in the Light." We are to turn from the darkness, face toward the Light, and walk in that Light.

When we confess our sins, we break the cycle of sin in our lives. However, we must make a willful determination to turn our backs on that sin and to respond to the Light of God. We make a choice to respond to God's holiness. It is a desire to be transparent and sincere in our relationship with and before God. We have nothing to hide, and we turn our backs on self-deception and manipulation.

To "walk in the Light" is not a declaration of our perfection. To say that we are "walking in the Light" does not mean that we have come to a point in our Christian experience where sin is no longer an issue in our lives. If that were the case, then John would have not added the words "and the blood of Jesus His Son cleanses us from all sin"— a clear implication that Jesus' blood continues to cleanse the confessing believers of the sins we continue to commit.

To "walk in the Light" simply means, first, to willingly expose our lives to God's brilliant Light, His holiness. Second, it means we must unhesitatingly respond in confession and repentance to what He exposes. Although sin is never eradicated from our lives, I believe that the stronghold of addictive sin is broken when we walk in the Light.

Sin cannot stand light. Mushrooms grow when you keep them in the dark and you feed them garbage. In the same way, sin thrives when it is shielded from the Light of God and fed the garbage of disobedience. That's why many Christians will reach some crisis point in dealing with a sin that controls them and cry out in sincere confession to the Lord, but then find themselves slipping back into the very sin they confessed. *The problem is that they have not come to the place where they are willing to do whatever it takes to overcome that sin.* Occasionally they are broken *by* the sin, but they have not broken *from* the sin. That requires walking in the Light.

I know a Christian woman who has struggled for years with telling the truth. Her habitual lying has eroded her integrity. It has caused her to lose friends. Even her family members don't take her seriously. Through the years she has been confronted by those who love her concerning her lies and dishonesty. On most of those occasions, she has responded by confessing her sin. But in between the confrontations she hides from accountability. So it isn't long before she slips back to her old ways. There is indeed evidence in her life that she knows the Lord, but she is not willing to make a clean break with this habit and stay in the Light.

Accountability is a wonderful and biblical tool to help you keep walking in the Light. Usually when fellow believers withdraw from other Christians, it's a telltale sign that something bad is going on. At the very least, the body of Christ is being robbed of the daily encouragement and power that comes from walking in the Light with brothers and sisters.

As Christians we possess the Light of God. When we are walking in fellowship with the Lord, others who are pursuing this kind of honest, transparent relationship are attracted to His Light shining through us. People who aren't pursuing that close relationship with God tend to avoid those who are. They simply don't want to be exposed by God's Light on their own or in a group, and for that reason they are not willing to do whatever it takes to stay in the Light.

Cultivating this honest, transparent relationship with God, His Light, and His people is what I mean by the "process of repentance." Confession of sin points us in the right direction. Walking in the Light accelerates our progress and holiness.

Let's not forget that we are on a journey—a journey to biblical wholeness—and our ultimate destination is to be in the presence of God. So right now we must focus on pursuing purity and holiness. Indeed, because we have given our lives to Christ, we have entered into a partnership with Him. We are related to God through Christ Jesus. This partnership and relationship must reflect the Light of His holiness.

That means we have to make it our business to deal directly and specifically with sin. We must turn from it and walk toward the Light. This is repentance, in point and process.

CHAPTER ELEVEN

The Long Way Home

There's an old saying, "Experience may not always be the best teacher, but it is the only school a fool will attend."

"Greg" grew up in a wonderful Christian family. At an early age he gave his life to Christ. All through grade school and middle school, Greg was an above-average student. There wasn't so much as a hint that there were any problems with his behavior.

But something happened to Greg when he entered high school. His grades began to slip. His parents noticed the lack of motivation. He lost interest in church activities. He began to hang out with a group of kids who had a pretty bad reputation around the school and in the community. He began to experiment with drugs and alcohol. Greg became increasingly disrespectful to his parents, and finally he had several brushes with the law.

Greg's parents were at their wits' end. They simply didn't know what to do. They had tried everything. Nothing seemed to wake Greg up. Greg's parents took away privileges, went through family counseling, and even sent him to live with some relatives that he greatly respected. Their hope was that these relatives would be able to talk some sense into their son. Although there were brief moments of change, in a few days Greg would go back to his patterns of rebellion and self-destructive behavior.

People even confronted Greg about his behavior on the basis of his Christian faith. But Greg had a common response to those confrontations: "Yes, I know what the Bible says. I am a Christian. But right now, I'm going to live my life the way I want to live it."

Poor grades and all of the trouble he got into guaranteed that he wasn't going to graduate from high school, so midway through his senior year he dropped out. After Greg's eighteenth birthday later that spring, his parents asked him to leave. He rented an apartment with a few of his friends. He periodically contacted his parents, usually when he needed money. But they were committed to exercising tough love. They refused his requests for money. They fully realized that they would be financing his irresponsible behavior.

Greg became angry and bitter. He was more determined than ever to live his life his way. His parents and friends prayed fervently for Greg. They prayed that somehow God would get through to his increasingly hardened heart. But by this time Greg was no longer casually smoking marijuana; he was a full-blown cocaine addict. He did anything to support his habit. He lost his job at a convenience store, got kicked out of his apartment, and his stubborn pride would not allow him to apologize to his parents and get the help that he needed.

God, too, was out of the picture. So Greg bounced around. He stayed temporarily at the homes of people who felt sorry for him. But soon they would find things missing, and Greg was back out on the streets.

Greg had completely worn out his welcome with his family, friends, and acquaintances alike. He had no place to go. Desperate to support his drug habit, he began to take more risks with his stealing. Late one Friday evening, Greg and two of his friends held up a convenience store.

During that robbery, something went terribly wrong. Greg had a gun. He directed the man behind the counter to empty the cash register. After the man gave him the money, Greg thought he saw the man reach underneath the counter. Greg panicked and shot the man. He and his friends ran from the scene. The man died.

Greg and his companions were caught by the police. Greg was convicted of his crimes, and he is now serving life in prison. But God used that tragedy to break through to Greg. During a visit by his parents shortly after he was arrested, the shame, the unconditional love of his parents, and the Bible verses he had memorized as a young child drove him to deep, heartfelt repentance. He begged his parents to forgive him. Of course, they did.

Greg, his parents, and virtually all of those who know him are greatly saddened by the events of Greg's life these past few years. Yet in Greg's own words, "I am so very sorry for the pain I have caused and the damage I have done to myself and to others. I don't want to be here in prison, but if it took [prison] to bring me back to the Lord, then I praise God for it."

Greg had to take the long, hard way home. It is absolutely miraculous that God spared his life. Admittedly, Greg's story is dramatic. Most of us have never traveled this route—but there are varying degrees of "Greg" in all of us.

REBELLION AND RESULTS

In short, some people have to learn things the hard way. Warnings are not good enough. Examples of others whose lives have been shipwrecked by disobedience don't move them. Confrontation won't correct them. Preaching and instruction fill their heads, but they refuse to change their ways. These people have to go through the heart-

wrenching, painful process of experiencing the consequences of disobedience and rebellion.

If they are Christians, then they are prime candidates
for God's discipline.

> You have not yet resisted to the point of shedding
> blood in your striving against sin; and you have forgot-
> ten the exhortation which is addressed to you as sons,
> "My son, do not regard lightly the discipline of the Lord,
> nor faint when you are reproved by Him; for those whom
> the Lord loves He disciplines, and He scourges every
> son whom He receives."
>
> It is for discipline that you endure; God deals with
> you as with sons; for what son is there whom his father
> does not discipline? But if you are without discipline, of
> which all have become partakers, then you are illegiti-
> mate children and not sons. Furthermore, we had earth-
> ly fathers to discipline us, and we respected them; shall
> we not much rather be subject to the Father of spirits,
> and live? For they disciplined us for a short time as
> seemed best to them, but He disciplines us for our good,
> so that we may share His holiness. All discipline for the
> moment seems not to be joyful, but sorrowful; yet to
> those who have been trained by it, afterwards it yields
> the peaceful fruit of righteousness. (Hebrews 12:4–11)

God does discipline His children! How we respond to
His discipline, then, is a crucial aspect of becoming a
whole person. We need to see God's discipline as a necessary marker on the way home rather than a needless intru-
sion on our personal freedom.

Rebellion is part of our fallen, sinful nature. Some people are more rebellious than others. Some are generally rebellious, and God's discipline is guiding them to a more
defined pathway of behavior. Others are more calculated in
their rebellion. They have an area of sin that they continue

to give in to. They refuse to respond to God's gracious invitations and warnings to "come home" and make things right. They know that what they are doing is wrong, but they enjoy it. They want it, and they sacrifice their fellowship with God to pursue it. They may pretend to others that everything is in order, but they know it is not.

I believe that more people in our churches and Christian organizations fall into this category of "calculated and hidden" rebellion than we realize. Others whose sin has been exposed still refuse, at least for the time being, to repent. Their rebellion is obvious. In either case, whether their rebellion is hidden or exposed, these people are the reason the Bible gives the story of the Prodigal Son.

THE LONG WAY HOME

Luke 15:11–24 tells the familiar story of the Prodigal Son. This story has been preached as an evangelistic message to encourage people to give their lives to Christ. (It is one of my evangelistic messages too!) Yet I believe that there is also a profound message in this story for Christians who have left the fellowship of our heavenly Father to pursue their selfish desires. This is the story of a young man who had to learn the hard way. He had to take the long way home. It is a story of rebellion, results, repentance, and reconciliation.

First, the story of the Prodigal Son is a story of rebellion. The story begins with a declaration of independence by the younger of two sons: "A man had two sons. The younger of them said to his father, 'Father, give me the share of the estate that falls to me.' So he divided his wealth between them."

It is interesting to me that Jesus did not mention any confrontation between the young man and the father. All Jesus offered is an account of a demand and the response to that demand. Perhaps there *had* been ongoing disagreements between the father and son. It could have been, then, that this father believed his young son needed to come face-to-face with the world of reality and consequences. Perhaps Dad had had enough of the squabbles and the battles of the wills, and he was ready to let the boy do what he wanted to do. The younger son could have been out of control—his subsequent behavior seems to support this—and his selfishness was a disruption to the peace and stability of the household.

For whatever reason, Dad had come to the end of the line. He gave his younger boy exactly what he had asked for and stepped aside. It was as if he said, "I will no longer stand in the way of what you want to do with your life. Here's the money. Enjoy the fruit of your selfishness. Have at it."

I am reminded of King Saul, who was repeatedly warned by God through the prophet Samuel to repent, get his act together, and obey God. But Saul wouldn't do it. So God turned Saul loose. He removed His blessing from Saul and gave the kingdom to David.

Sin is powerful and deceptive. It was the same in Saul's case as it was with the Prodigal Son—and is in ours. Once we are addicted to sin, it makes us its slave. Paul made this truth quite clear: "Do you not know that when you present yourselves to someone as slaves for obedience, you are slaves of the one whom you obey, either of sin resulting in death, or of obedience resulting in righteousness?" (Romans 6:16).

Sin even fills us with a false sense of joy. It gives us momentary pleasure. Yet people of faith learn to refuse this short-lived benefit: "By faith Moses, when he had grown up, refused to be called the son of Pharaoh's daughter, choosing rather to endure ill-treatment with the people of God than to enjoy the passing pleasures of sin" (Hebrews 11:24–25).

Here's the problem: Because sin blinds us with its false sense of fulfillment, we lie to ourselves. We are driven to ignore the coming payday of sin's results. We somehow think that the consequences will not catch up to us. We tend to believe that our gracious and merciful heavenly Father will soften the blow and not allow us to reap what we have sown. Therefore, we willfully push ahead and do what we want to do.

That's where we pick up the story of the Prodigal Son again. With newfound freedom and a pocketful of money, this young man got as far away from home as he could. He did everything he felt like doing. He had no boundaries and no accountability, and nobody knew who he was. He could indulge himself to the maximum: "And not many days later, the younger son gathered everything together and went on a journey into a distant country, and there he squandered his estate with loose living" (Luke 15:13).

Make no mistake here: This boy was completely out of control and loving every sinful minute. He was like the alcoholic who finds the keys to the liquor store. He completely abandoned any sense of responsibility to God, his parents, and even himself.

But this young man was not really free. In fact, in a perverse way, he was demonstrating his slavery to sin. That's the explanation for his apparent inability to break free from the stranglehold that sin and selfishness had over him, even when it became apparent that he would self-destruct. Sin drove him to irresponsible behavior and whispered in his ear, "Do all that you want to do and do it now!"

I have a friend who told me that a number of years ago he took a major spiritual "vacation." He did almost every sinful thing that would cross his mind. I asked, "So what were you thinking about while you did all this stuff?"

My friend minced no words. "Crawford, I knew that I was wrong, but I just could not stop. I became a slave to sin."

I have known Christians (including pastors, missionaries, and Christian leaders) who have lived in adulterous re lationships for years while publicly denouncing the very sin that they continue to commit. They are "hidden" prodigals who have become slaves to sin—and God always deals with sin.

THE CONSEQUENCES OF
NEGLECTING THE ROAD HOME

Sin never has gone unpunished and never will. There are *consequences* to what we do. The story of the Prodigal Son is a powerful picture of this unalterable biblical truth. You see, secondly, this is a story of results. Weigh these sobering words from Luke 15:14–16:

> Now when he had spent everything, a severe famine occurred in that country, and he began to be impoverished. So he went and hired himself out to one of the citizens of that country, and he sent him into his fields to feed swine. And he would have gladly filled his stomach with the pods that the swine were eating, and no one was giving anything to him.

He was hemmed in. The walls were closing in. He was in a fix. He had blown all of his money. He was probably without friends, since his relationships were probably determined by how much he had in his pockets. To add insult to injury, he was in a strange country, a long way from home, and in the middle of an unanticipated famine.

You would think that this would be his wake-up call. Wouldn't you think that at this point he'd face the music, contact his dad, and somehow try to get back home? But that's not the case. Out of sheer desperation he begged a pig farmer to give him a job feeding the hogs. The man gave him the job, but nothing to eat.

Remember, the Prodigal Son was from a Jewish family. He was reduced to feeding some of the most detestable animals to a Jew—swine. The swine were fed, but the Prodigal

Son was left with nothing. What a frightening picture of what unrepented sin does to us! We feed sin and we are left to starve spiritually. The wages of sin is always death.

Sin, pride, stubbornness, and deception are all related. They produce a spiritual insanity in us that keeps us from facing the truth about ourselves, about God, and about our circumstances. I have met people who would rather face destruction than humble themselves, admit that they are wrong, and do what it takes to make things right. Sometimes they think that their wit and willpower will get them through. Other times, they have a perverted view of the grace and mercy of God. Their thinking goes something like this: *Because God loves me, He is going to get me out of this. He knows that I'm only human. He knows that I sin like everybody else does. He's going to help me.*

But their cry for mercy is not accompanied with repentance. God reaches a point at which He no longer responds to our sinful insincerity. He actually closes His ears to our prayers, according to Psalm 66:18: "If I regard wickedness in my heart, the Lord will not hear."

God will then act in discipline and judgment—and, as the writer of Hebrews said, "It is a terrifying thing to fall into the hands of the living God" (Hebrews 10:31).

God has made provision for us to deal with sin, but He will not tolerate sin. There comes a point at which God will not only refuse to respond to our insincerity, but He will also become proactive in dealing with our disobedience.

In certain instances, God will bring about premature death to those who will not respond to His discipline and invitations to repent. Look at these startling words in 1 John 5:16–17:

> If anyone sees his brother committing a sin not leading to death, he shall ask and God will for him give life to those who commit sin not leading to death. There is a sin leading to death; I do not say that he should make

request for this. All unrighteousness is sin, and there is a sin not leading to death.

The expression "sin leading to death," in my view, does not refer to a specific sin that would require physical death but rather the state of continuous, repeated, unrepented sin. It is the flagrant disregard of God's warnings and the rejection of His call to repent. It results in the dishonoring of God's name and reputation by those who are His children. And it seems that sometimes God says that He has had enough and will take that person out of this life.

I don't mean to suggest that every young person who dies, or every Christian who experiences a sudden death, has been living in sin. Ultimately, only God knows for sure the person who has "sinned unto death." But I believe that I have witnessed this act of judgment on at least two occasions. One of the young men to whom I referred in a previous chapter rejected repeated warnings to break off the affair in which he was involved, and then he died in a tragic accident. Another situation involved a pastor who wrongfully divorced his wife and married another woman. Shortly thereafter, he died of a heart attack.

I will say again, only God knows about these two situations with certainty. Still, the point is that God does not play with sin. When we do not walk in, and respond to, the provision He has made for our sin, then we are on our own.

The Prodigal Son had reached the dangerous bottom. What would he do? How would he respond? Would he embrace the truth about himself and his condition, or would he continue to "gut it out" and allow his self-centered rebellion to drive him to final disaster?

What about you? Have you become casual and callous about sin in your life? Have you been paying attention to God's warnings and His call for you to walk away from rebellion? Are you ready to experience repentance and complete restoration? Or have you been putting off your response and holding on to prideful excuses for not coming home spiritually?

If this is your description, your heart will become increasingly hardened. Your will to respond to God will continue to erode. You're headed for sure disaster. Don't you want to change? Now, *right now,* is the time to do business with God. No more running. No more excuses. No more hiding. Put away the lies and the head games.

Face the truth about yourself and your condition, and God will meet you right where you are.

CHAPTER TWELVE

The Way Home: Repentance and Reconciliation

M y friend Steve was a lifeguard in his younger years. He told me the story of a young girl named Gidget, who was a bit of a tomboy. Steve had taught Gidget to swim a few years before. Gidget had become so accomplished a swimmer that she was part of the town's American Athletic Union swimming team. She played herself up as kind of a tough cookie. Gidget was very independent, and she made it clear to everyone around her that she—at the age of ten—could handle herself in the water.

As he was watching over the deep end of the community pool one bright July afternoon, my friend noticed Gidget preparing for her first dive from the high diving board. Gidget was a pure joy to watch on the one-meter board. She was compact and athletic enough that she could flip, pike, or somersault to her heart's content from that board.

But the three-meter board—that was different. Gidget stood in line waiting for her turn, and she somberly made her way up the ladder to the diving springboard. She hesitated at the top, then made her way to the middle of the board. Once there, she froze.

"Gidget," Steve called out over the splashing and voices of the pool. "Gidget, you don't have to dive if you don't want to." That may have been the wrong thing to say. Gidget walked to the edge of the board with a defiant look at Steve. Then she froze again.

"Are you sure you want to do this now?" Steve was trying to give her some kind of out. Permission to go back down the board would save her some face. Gidget nodded, but never looked again at Steve. She looked down at the water, gulped, and leaped off the board.

She never really decided whether she wanted to enter the water feetfirst or headfirst. Steve says that if ever a "10" should be given for a belly flop, Gidget deserved it that day.

Gidget sank under the pool surface, never having moved a muscle from her belly-flop position. Steve actually had the opportunity to blow his whistle, do the classic spread-eagle jump from his lifeguard tower, and dive down after her.

The whole process only took a few seconds. As soon as they broke the surface, Gidget spoke to Steve. She was still trying to recover from having the wind completely knocked out of her. "I . . . don't . . . need . . . your . . . help."

So Steve said, "Have it your way. I'll swim beside you, just in case." Then he let go of her.

She sank again. Steve barely let her head go under before he brought her back to the surface. She spoke again. "Changed . . . my . . . mind." This time, she let Steve take her to the side of the pool and rest.

Gidget's decision came when she realized she wasn't strong enough on her own to make it to the side of the pool. The Prodigal Son's moment of decision came when he realized he wasn't strong enough to make it on his own, having crashed into the pool of the consequences of his decisions.

COMING TO YOUR SENSES

This is the third feature of this story. This is a story of repentance. Repentance finally happened in the prodigal when he got the message of his circumstances:

> But when he came to his senses, he said, "How many of my father's hired men have more than enough bread, but I am dying here with hunger! I will get up and go to my father, and will say to him, 'Father, I have sinned against heaven, and in your sight; I am no longer worthy to be called your son; make me as one of your hired men.'" So he got up and came to his father. *(Luke 15:17–20a)*

Finally, here's some sound reasoning from the Prodigal Son. He actually figured out that it didn't make sense for him to be starving and homeless. It's as if he said, "I'm not without options. I can humble myself, walk away from this mess, and go back home to a safe place."

As long as we are breathing, we have two options: our way or God's way. Proverbs 14:12 spells out the results of our way: "There is a way which seems right to a man, but its end is the way of death."

Thank God! The Prodigal Son chose God's way. But also notice that the pride and arrogance are gone. His rebellious, demanding spirit is replaced with a broken, grateful heart. Second, he fully owns the fact and responsibility of his sin.

These are indeed two of the three characteristics of true repentance. Some people say all of the right words but are not genuinely repentant. It's kind of like the husband who has offended his wife and knows that he is wrong. He acknowledges the offense and asks for forgiveness, but she can tell that he is insincere and he is not truly sorry. He just wants to get off the hot seat—but he only gets into hot water.

God seeks our acknowledgment of personal responsibility for sin, accompanied by genuine sorrow concerning the sinful act or behavior. Some argue that emotions have nothing to do with repentance. I disagree. All sin is a matter of the heart, not just an act of the brain. Simply changing your *mind* about your sin does not mean that you're going to change your *heart* and redirect your *will* to do the right thing.

That's why the apostle Paul said in 2 Corinthians 7:9–10,

> I now rejoice, not that you were made sorrowful, but that you were made sorrowful to the point of repentance; for you were made sorrowful according to the will of God, so that you might not suffer loss in anything through us. For the sorrow that is according to the will of God produces a repentance without regret, leading to salvation, but the sorrow of the world produces death.

Again, the repentant person must have godly sorrow and brokenness concerning sin. I'm not suggesting that we identify some list of acceptable, appropriate emotional responses that would serve as indications of true repentance. But I *am* saying that the person must have a sense of remorse, a heartfelt sorrow, for the hurt that sin causes to God and to others.

A few years ago here in Atlanta two men committed a heinous, brutal crime. They kidnaped a young woman in her early twenties. They held her hostage for several days. They repeatedly raped and beat her. They then took her to a wooded area, where one of the men took a shotgun and literally blew her head off her shoulders.

A few weeks later, the two men were captured and put under arrest. Portions of the trial were broadcast on local television. I will never forget looking at the hard, cold faces of those men as the judge issued their sentences. The triggerman received the death penalty. Then the judge confirmed what practically everyone knew when he said, "Throughout this trial, I've looked for even the slightest evidence of remorse or sorrow— *and I have found none.*"

The Prodigal Son not only knew that what he had done was wrong, he was sorry for the wrong that he had done. In fact, he was sorry enough to do what was right. I guess that's really the issue when it comes to repentance, isn't it? In other words, we may have degrees of sorrow concerning our sin, but are we sorry enough to change? Are we ready to turn around, walk away from our sin, and seek to make things right?

There were probably many times the prodigal had felt twinges of guilt but chose to ignore the feelings. Desperate circumstances had to erase every shred of his optimism about his self-directed path. Then his guilt burst through like a tidal wave. At that point, he was sorry enough to change.

What about you? Is there unrepented sin in your life? Are you controlling the guilt or managing the sin, or are you sorry enough to change? Acknowledging your sin and feeling remorse is two-thirds of the way home. There is a third element to repentance: Repentance also involves the will. Just as there is willful rebellion, there must also be willful repentance. Repentance is something that we *do,* not just something that we feel or think.

MAKING IT HOME

Acknowledgment and sincerity have never changed anyone's life. They drive us to change, but ultimately change takes place through an act of the will. It is when we follow through and make the about-face to walk away from our sin and toward the Lord that the cycle of repentance has been completed. And that's what Jesus said that the Prodigal Son did. Look at these sweet words in Luke 15:20: "So he got up and came to his father."

I suppose the boy could have stayed there on that pig

farm weeping and beating himself up about how bad things were, how awful and irresponsible he had been, and how terrible a son he had become. But that would only have amounted to depression and self-destruction. *Feeling the pain and the consequences of your sin will not necessarily lead to repentance.* In fact, the sorrow could become so great that it emotionally paralyzes you, hindering you from what must be done to overcome the sin. You could even begin to think that your sin is greater than the grace of God.

Some years ago, a man planted a church. He was known for both his tremendous passion for the Lord and his love for people. He was a gifted preacher and evangelist. The church grew rapidly. In a few years, it became a model for other churches to follow. Things were going great—and then it was discovered that their beloved pastor was having an affair.

When the pastor was confronted with the situation, he confessed that it was indeed true. He stood before the church, tearfully acknowledged his sin, and resigned. He was overcome by shame and grief. He left the ministry, moved out of town, and shut off all contact with friends at the church.

Some years later on a Sunday morning, I preached in that very church without knowing any of this. During the course of my message, I felt particularly led to emphasize God's grace, forgiveness, and unconditional love. When I finished preaching, I gave an invitation for those who needed to experience this wonderful love and acceptance to come forward. Many responded. It was a "God moment." My attention was especially drawn to a man in his sixties who was literally on his face at the altar, sobbing and pounding his fist into the carpet, saying repeatedly, "God, I'm so sorry. God, I'm so sorry."

I prayed with him and spent time with him after the service. I found out that he was the founding pastor. That morning had been his first time back in the church since he had resigned. For years this gentle man of God had carried with him the guilt, shame, and sorrow of his sin. It had driven him to depression, destroyed his marriage, and imprisoned him in isolation and loneliness. That day, he was returning to the church because he wanted to walk away from his guilt and put an end to the pain. Simply put, he wanted to come home.

I often think of that man and the vivid scene at the altar that Sunday morning. I don't know where he is today or what happened after our conversation. But I will never forget the lesson that was underscored in my soul that day: An unhealthy, hopeless sorrow will take us to the wrong place. God's sorrow, the conviction of the Holy Spirit, always leads us to repentance and restoration—not to isolation and destruction.

God loves us. He wants to pour out that love and grace on us. But we have to allow the guilt and sorrow that we feel to move us toward our loving heavenly Father and not to keep us stuck in self-pity. Ultimately, that's the point of the story of the Prodigal Son.

One more thing: This is a story of reconciliation. Repentance says that there's no such thing as irreconcilable differences. When we meet God's requirements concerning our sin, the issue is finished. We are reunited in fellowship with the Father. We are at home and at peace. God even gives us a "Welcome Home!" party. Read the moving way in which Jesus described the response of this father to his rebellious but now repentant son:

> But while he was still a long way off, his father saw him and felt compassion for him, and ran and embraced him and kissed him. And the son said to him, "Father, I have sinned against heaven and in your sight; I am no longer worthy to be called your son." But the father said to his slaves, "Quickly bring out the best robe and put it on him, and put a ring on his hand and sandals on his feet;

and bring the fattened calf, kill it, and let us eat and celebrate; for this son of mine was dead and has come to
life again; he was lost and has been found." And they
began to celebrate. *(Luke 15:20b–24)*

This is a stunning picture of God's response to us when
we turn to Him from our sin. Notice there is no lecture, no
"I told you so," no statement suggesting, "Since you left,
why don't you find someplace else to live?" Not at all. Just
the opposite.

It's as if the father said, "I never wanted you to leave,
but something in you drove you away. I have been looking
every day for you to walk down the lane to our house. You
don't know how many times the tears have flooded my
eyes as I have prayed for you and wondered, 'How's my
son?' There's nothing I wouldn't do for you. In fact, right
now let's have a party to demonstrate my love for you!"

Every prodigal child needs to understand that God is
waiting for us to come home. He has made every provision
for us to return to Him. He is not standing waiting to dish
out punishment. He won't place a sign around your neck
that says, "This person failed Me." The same grace He
showered on us when we received Christ as our Savior and
Lord awaits us when we walk away from our sin and rebellion and decide to come home.

God is waiting to wrap His arms around you and to tell
you, "I forgive you. It's OK. I love you." The truth of the
matter is, God never stops loving us. We can't make God
love us more. No matter what we do, He will never love us
less, even though we wandered from Him and did shame-
ful things.

That's right. No matter where you are in your process of
making it home before dark, you can still count on God's
unfailing, unchanging, incomprehensible love.

I have a very good friend who had been a drug addict
for fourteen years. Then he became a Christian, and God

delivered him from his addiction. Years later, while he was in seminary preparing for the ministry, the temptation to get high revisited him with a vengeance.

He fell. He began to use drugs again. But he sought help, repented, and went through a drug rehabilitation program. He'll be the first to tell you that his road back home was filled with self-doubt and shame. But he said that the turning point came one day when he was sitting at home, so ashamed of himself for what he had done and so hurt for the people he had let down that he couldn't stop crying.

Then all of a sudden he kept hearing a voice say, "I love you. I love you. I love you." It was at that point, he says, that he began to take his eyes off his failure and accept the grace and unconditional love of God. His heavenly Father wrapped His arms around him and gave him a grace party.

And God will do the same for all of us when we come home.

CHAPTER THIRTEEN

From My Heart

Sin plagues all of us. To live an overcoming Christian life (or, in the words of others, a victorious Christian life) does not mean that we are ever at a place in our relationship with the Lord in which we are beyond the possibility of sinful failure. Sin is all around us. It is part of the atmosphere of our fallen world. We cannot escape its devastation. It has touched us all. And in varying degrees, we all have at one point or the other struggled with its stranglehold on our lives. Yes, even now we are working on keeping it and its influence away from us (or at least we should be). Repentance is God's means and our only solution to dealing with sin, the plague of humanity. And, as I have tried to point out, repentance is not just something that we do; it is who we are; it is our identity. We are repenters.

At the core of repentance is the admission that we are inadequate, insufficient, needy people who cannot make it unless God intervenes on our behalf. To repent is to confess that we have failed and that we are capable of—no, even drawn to—a lifestyle of sinful failure if the grace, mercy, and strong arm of God do not snatch us and hold us. Let me say it again: We are only sustained by the grace of God! We experience deliverance from sin and victory over sin when we are aware of how absolutely inadequate and dependent we are.

The American church is in danger of losing this perspective. I am troubled and saddened over the self-righteous pronouncements and posturing that is becoming increasingly characteristic of our flavor of Christianity in this country. Some churches, Christian schools, and Christian organizations have contributed to the erection of spiritual walls, under the false and unbiblical assumption that the best way to affect non-Christians is to create our own world, occasionally tossing a Gospel grenade over the wall and at the same time making sure that we denounce *their* lifestyles, beliefs, and worldview.

This artificial separation has fed our pride. We set ourselves up for the selective denunciation of sin. We find it easier to point to and eloquently address the sins of the "unbelieving culture" than we do our sins, the sins of the church. This was the disease of the Pharisees (Luke 11:37–40), and it is becoming our ailment too.

God intended for us to interact with and relate to non-Christians. Obviously this is the only way we can fulfill our Lord's mission for our lives (Matthew 28:18–20). Further, it is impossible to affect that with which we do not come in contact. When we interact with unbelievers, not only do we become "salt" and "light" (Matthew 5:13–16), but unbelievers become God's mirrors, His loving reminders of His grace and forgiveness that He has so abundantly and freely poured out on us (Luke 7:36–50). Our interaction with nonbelievers keeps biblical Christianity in perspective. In other words, when we are actively engaged in sharing the hope and love of Christ with an unbelieving world, we are likely to be drawn away from a self-centered, petty perspective on our relationship with God. Our hearts will be filled afresh with gratitude to God that we have been cleansed. We will also be aware that we still stand in need of cleansing.

MOVING BACK TO HIGHER GROUND

I believe that the church needs to be called back to the high ground of holiness. In recent years we have spent a lot of time preaching and teaching on the practical aspects of the Christian life. The shelves in our Christian bookstores are filled with books on everything from how to manage our time to a Christian approach to dieting. We have conferences and seminars on handling our anger, managing our money, and setting goals and achieving them. Let me quickly say I believe it is important to have a distinctively Christian worldview and to have a clear, practical approach to Christian living. In fact, I believe in relevant, practical, biblical preaching that helps people deal with the daily struggles and challenges of the Christian life. But as I have tried to make clear in this book, the process is not the destination. We can get so preoccupied with the "how to's" that we forget that the person of Christ is the Christian life.

We have been called not just to do Christianity but to be distinctively Christian. God's mandate for us is to demonstrate to the world what, by the grace of God, people can become when we allow Him to cleanse us from our sins. He is looking for a church that is passionately pursuing purity; a community of people who are embracing an authentic relationship with Him and who care more about their spiritual integrity and godliness than they do about occupying positions of "influence" and winning the latest national debate. Yes, I believe we as Christians have a moral obligation to represent Christ in our world by engaging the culture and presenting a Christian view on the significant issues facing the culture, but never at the expense of a transparent pure desire to both articulate and demonstrate the hope of Christ and a holy life. The burden is squarely on our shoulders.

I believe that when we pursue this kind of pure relationship with Him, He will visit us in mighty revival and bring in an abundant harvest of souls. But judgment begins at the house of God.

When we work on cleaning up our own mess, we become the compelling models of God's work in the world. God's method throughout history has been not only to denounce sin but also to provide a visible example of what He is looking for. The incarnation is the ultimate expression of the utter integrity of God. Look at that great verse, John 1:14, "And the Word became flesh, and dwelt among us, and we saw His glory, glory as of the only begotten from the Father, full of grace and truth." Precious, powerful words!

LIVING IN THE WORLD

Think about it. When God wanted to redeem us, reestablishing our relationship with Him and proving His love for us, He did not just utter words, but He sent His Son, *the Word,* to visibly demonstrate His intentions. Jesus modeled grace and truth before our very eyes. He is God's living object lesson.

We too are called to be incarnational Christians. Our lives must back up what we say. They must not be glaring contradictions of the integrity of the Gospel we proclaim. And God has given us His precious Holy Spirit to produce this kind of holy authenticity in and through our lives. His Spirit indeed empowers us to clean up the sinful messes in our lives.

I love Luke's account of the Great Commission. Jesus said in Luke 24:49, "And behold, I am sending forth the promise of My Father upon you; but you are to stay in the city until you are clothed with power from on high." These words from Jesus foreshadow the words and events of Acts chapters one and two, when the Spirit of God came upon the followers of Christ.

It is a mistake, though, to view these passages as primarily emphasizing the Holy Spirit's role in the strategic spread and proclamation of the Gospel. Look again at Luke 24:49. Notice the expression "clothed with power." The word "clothed" means to take on the appearance of another. And the word translated "power" is the Greek word *dunamis*. This word can be translated "inherent ability." The point is that Jesus wanted His followers to experience the complete transforming power of the Holy Spirit. When the Holy Spirit controls our lives, we are changed and we become agents for change (Acts 1:8). We don't just speak the truth of the Gospel; our lives become the visible demonstration of the truth of the Gospel. This is what I mean by incarnational, authentic Christianity. The Holy Spirit cleanses and purifies us of sin so that our lips and our lives tell the truth about Christ. It is one complete package.

This is the wholeness and the holiness that our souls must long for. And it is this kind of wholehearted devotion that brings the blessing and favor of God. I love 2 Chronicles 16:9, "For the eyes of the Lord move to and fro throughout the earth that He may strongly support those whose heart is completely His." When we become what God is looking for, then He rushes to us, not only to give us His strength, but also to point others to Himself through us! Repentance places us in a position for God's favor.

This is why repentance is so crucial. Failure to repent launches us on the path to hypocrisy and self-righteousness, and it may confirm us in a cultural Christianity that mars the name and reputation of our Savior. The call of Christ is a call to face and embrace the truth about who He is and who we are. Yes! We will discover that there is a huge gap between who we are and who He is. But repentance—constant, continuous repentance—bridges the gap. Our lives shout to the watching world that He is real, and God's own heart is drawn toward us. He, through the person of the Holy Spirit, then empowers us and gives us all that we need to be overcomers. From us will flow "rivers of living water" (John 7:38) to quench our thirst and the thirst of those with whom we come in contact.

I began this book by quoting the prayer, "Let Me Make It Home Before Dark," by my dear friend and mentor, Robertson McQuilkin. I have the privilege of serving on the board of trustees of Columbia International University, the school where Dr. McQuilkin served as president for many years. His dear wife, Muriel, suffers from Alzheimer's disease. As her health declined, Dr. McQuilkin felt it was his responsibility and, in his words, his privilege to devote his time and attention to caring for his life partner. So he resigned as president. I was at the board meeting when he announced his resignation and read the prayer. There was not a dry eye in the room. As he read the prayer we all knew that it was his prayer request that he would finish the journey down here strong and well. His words gripped my heart that day. For I, too, do not want to bring shame or dishonor to my Savior and betray the trust and confidence of the "great cloud of witnesses" who surround me and are cheering me on.

Since that board meeting I have found myself paying closer attention to areas of weakness and making Paul's words in 1 Corinthians 9:24–27 my goal and fervent prayer request. I want to be tied to His heart, and repentance keeps me walking toward home.

As I write these words I am in New Jersey, the state in which I was born and where I spent the first eighteen years of my life. The other day I visited the church where I trusted Christ as a teenager. No one but the secretary was there, and after I told her who I was, she let me in. I walked into the sanctuary and stood at the altar where more than thirty years ago I surrendered my life to Jesus Christ.

I then drove a few blocks to my old neighborhood. As I sat in the car in front of the house where our family used to live, I thought of my parents, who are both in heaven. I remember the love and confidence that they showered on me and my dad's frequent admonition to me: "Boy, do right!"

I pulled away from the house and drove about ten miles to the campus of the small college where I spent my freshman year. When I turned into the campus, I spotted the small chapel where I often went to pray between classes or during the lunch hour. God reminded me of how He met me during those sweet intimate times of worship and communion with Him. He reminded me that He had answered my prayers that He would use me and keep me. I began to weep.

And once again my heart was flooded with the goodness of God. I found myself crying out to God to help me to be faithful, to remember how far He has brought me, and to keep repentance as my friend and ally so I can make it home before dark.

And so I end the way we began. Take one more look at McQuilkin's prayer and make it your prayer.

"LET ME GET HOME BEFORE DARK"

It's sundown, Lord. The shadows of my life stretch back into the dimness of the years long spent. I fear not death, for that grim foe betrays himself at last, thrusting me forever into life: life with You, unsoiled and free. But I do fear. I fear the dark specter may come too soon—or do I mean too late? I fear that before I finish I might stain Your honor, shame Your name, grieve Your loving heart. Few, they tell me, finish well. Lord, let me get home before dark.

Will my life show the darkness of a spirit grown mean and small, fruit shriveled on the vine, bitter to the taste of my companions, a burden to be borne by those brave few who love me still? No. Lord, let the fruit grow lush and sweet, a joy to all who taste, a spirit-sign of God at work, stronger, fuller. Brighter at the end. Lord, let me get home before dark.

Will it be the darkness of tattered gifts, rust locked,

half-spent, or ill-spent, a life that once was used of God now set aside? Grief for glories gone or fretting for a task God never gave? Mourning in the hollow chambers of memory, gazing on the faded banners of victories long gone? Cannot I run well until the end? Lord, let me get home before dark.

The outer me decays—I do not fret or ask reprieve. The ebbing strength but weans me from mother earth and grows me up for heaven. I do not cling to shadows cast by mortality. I do not patch the scaffold lent to build the real, eternal me. I do not clutch about me my cocoon, vainly struggling to hold hostage a free spirit pressing to be born.

But will I reach the gate in lingering pain—body distorted, grotesque? Or will it be a mind wandering untethered among light phantasies or grim terrors? Of Your grace, Father, I humbly ask . . . let me get home before dark.

Is your faith low on passion?

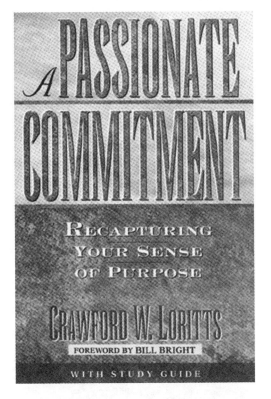

A Passionate Commitment
Recapturing Your Sense of Purpose

We got to church. We sing worship songs. We read our Bibles. So why do we feel so empty? The problem is that we've lost our sense of passion and purpose. This is a book to help us rekindle our spiritual spark and begin to live a life of inner joy, enthusiasm, and deep spiritual passion.

Quality Paperback 0-8024-5246-9

MOODY
The Name You Can Trust
1-800-678-8812 www.MoodyPress.org

Men: What does God require of you?

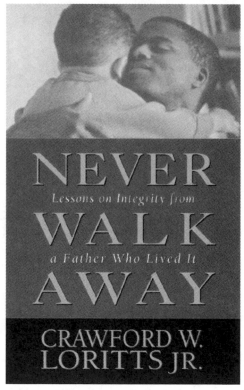

Never Walk Away
Lessons on Integrity from a Father Who Lived It

Each husband and father has the means to powerfully shape his family's future. By your example, you can instill in your children a standard for love that endures. Discover how you can exhibit faithfulness that will have a far-reaching impact on your kids as well as future generations.

Quality Paperback 0-8024-2742-1